The Liberation of a Resentful Wife

Carol Arnold

SUNNY
SunnyPublishers.com

Title: The Liberation of a Resentful Wife
Author: Carol L. Arnold
Publisher: Sunny Publishers
Editors: Dean W. Arnold and Daniel P. Bockert
Book Design and Typography: Daniel P. Bockert
Cover Design: Robbie Tipton

Copyright 2006 by Carol L. Arnold

ISBN 0-9749076-7-7

Sunny Publishers is an imprint of:
Chattanooga Historical Foundation Company
P.O. Box 2053, Chattanooga, Tennessee 37409
info@SunnyPublishers.com

To purchase more books, visit SunnyPublishers.com

To contact the author, e-mail Carol at:
DoctorJLA@hotmail.com

Comments regarding *The Liberation of a Resentful Wife:*

"My assistant has begged Carol for years to write this book. I personally discipled the author in the 1950s at UCLA where Bill and I started Crusade. Her teachings have been influential and empowering to women throughout the world."

> — *Vonette Bright*
> *Cofounder, Campus Crusade for Christ*

"Carol's influence reaches around the world today, but for me it is still close to home. Her wonderful example and insights inspired me to be a better wife and mom, and helped me prepare my daughter to take on her new role as wife. I highly recommend this book."

> — *Kay Coles James*
> *Author and former U.S. Assistant Secretary*
> *of Health and Human Services*

"God's amazing grace is sufficient to restore a broken marriage. The story of Jack and Carol Arnold's marriage is a beautiful picture of the power of the gospel."

> — *Susan Hunt*
> *Author of* By Design: God's Distinctive
> Calling for Women

Contents

Note to Readers

I WAS ASKED to write this book by women all over the world so they could hear my story again and share it with others who are struggling in their marriage. Apart from such persuasion, I would not have written this book.

I do not consider myself a writer. I would rather speak to large audiences than to put pen to paper.

This is not a theological book. I do strive to be biblically accurate in the following pages, but other works should be consulted for fuller treatments on the theology of marriage. This is my story—what I have learned and what has happened in my life. By telling it, my desire is to give other wives hope, encouragement, and perhaps a laugh or two.

My four sons—Mark, Brian, Arny, and Dean—have supported me in this effort, shared valuable insights, and given me the courage to write this book. I am grateful for their godly lives and the examples they are to my grandchildren.

—Carol Arnold
Orlando, Florida

To my four sons, their wives,
and their children.

Part I

The End of
My Marriage

MY HUSBAND dropped to the floor from a heart attack on January 9, 2005, while preaching to hundreds of people.

How did I feel about it? The answer is long and complex.

At least I was spared from actually watching the incident. Earlier that day, I had called my friend Mary Ann, who was signed up to watch the nursery.

"Would you like me to replace you? I've heard this message three times."

"I'd love that," she said. "I don't know when I'll get to hear Jack preach again."

While sitting in a rocking chair, holding an infant, I heard footsteps running down the hallway toward the nursery. I thought some kid was goofing off during church. A young man threw open the door and shouted at the woman next to me, a medically trained physician's assistant.

"Darlene, come quick!" he said. "Jack has collapsed in the pulpit."

The young man didn't see me there. As they ran off, I said to myself, "Well, I'd better go too."

My first thought was that I had fixed Jack a decent break-fast—eggs, juice, toast, and fruit. Our marriage had a pretty checkered past, but if there was one bit of consistency to the chaos, it was that I had always laid out the food on a regular basis. So why would he faint?

Our church met at the large, modern auditorium of Reformed Theological Seminary near Orlando, Florida. As I hurried to the stairs, the elevator doors popped open to my left, and several people gave me a serious, somber look. I began to sense that something more than a typical fainting had occurred.

On my way to the auditorium, a number of people were rush-ing out, talking on their cell phones in an urgent tone. When I entered, the rest of the congregation was bowed in prayer, except for a few people huddled by the podium surrounding a man on the floor. They were performing CPR.

⚜

FOR YEARS I had secretly resented my role as wife and "helper" to my husband. The resentment began two weeks after our wedding, when Jack would read at his desk, not in bed, to keep the light from bothering me. When I would try to entice him to come to bed, wearing a thin nightgown, he would just ask me to make him another cup of tea.

I got pregnant two months after the wedding—something we had not planned on. The understanding had been that I would work for four years to help put Jack through seminary. Now the future did not look like I had imagined. This crisis was followed by many more conflicts, and my resentment for Jack grew and continued for decades.

I reached the place where I was no longer in love with my husband. My desires were not to please him or to meet his needs. I was going through the motions of being a wife, fooling everybody but me and God.

Things were not so good between me and the pastor, but I was very good at being a pastor's wife. I taught a number of Bible studies. I traveled regularly as a featured speaker for the Christian Women's Club, sharing my conversion testimony at area country clubs. I got up early, studied the Scriptures, and underlined key passages with my special pencil—blue on one side, red on the other.

However, I was deceiving myself by thinking I could have a close walk with God when my relationship with my husband was terrible. I secretly resented my role as wife and helper to my husband.

Jack also looked as if nothing was wrong at home. Our church in Roanoke, Virginia, was growing, and building projects were underway. He spoke several times a week and even appeared on radio and TV at various times. But he was not getting his strokes at home, and many other formidable pressures closed in over time. The church split. Jack was hospitalized and diagnosed with clinical depression. He did not preach for several months. While he brought his own problems to the table, he was also the victim of difficult circumstances, but I had no compassion at all. "You need to snap out of it," was my general feeling, which I articulated many times.

I failed miserably in this relationship for many years, even though the first verses of the Bible say God created the wife to help the husband, to complement his weaknesses, to encourage and meet his needs, and to build him up.

One of the hardest lessons I had to learn was that I could no longer think of myself as a godly woman, filled with the Spirit and walking close to the Lord, if I was not being the kind of wife that God wanted me to be. I was willing to meet the needs of everyone on earth except the one for whom God had specifically created me.

God had to bring me to a place in my life where I saw my marriage crumbling and my children distressed, where I was forced to acknowledge I was no longer able—or even willing—to be the spiritual woman portrayed in the books and magazines. I hated going to marriage seminars. When we did go to counseling, I was able to place all the blame on my husband.

THIS WAS the same man whom I was now approaching after he had collapsed in the pulpit. While he lay on the floor, I inched up close to his body to see what had happened to him. He looked gone. I stepped back a few feet and turned my head away while the congregation prayed silently. I looked up again as the paramedics rushed in and put the 69-year-old preacher in the ambulance. I rode in the passenger seat, alone with my emotions, not knowing at the time that he had died instantly.

It would be a matter of hours before Jack's sensational death made national and international news. He had been preaching on heaven and had quoted his lifetime verse, Philippians 1:21, "For to me, to live is Christ and to die is gain." He also quoted John Wesley: "As long as God has work for me to do, I am immortal" and then Jack added, "but if my work is done, I'm outta here." Moments later he pointed upward and spoke his last words, "And when I go to heaven…" He stopped, grabbed the pulpit, swayed briefly, and fell backward.

"He was just all there, and then not there at all, like a hand came through the roof and snatched him out of his body," said an eyewitness who was sitting only five feet away from where Jack fell.

The story hit the AP wire and was listed by Yahoo as the most-read story of the day. A family friend from Sweden e-mailed us after seeing the report on CNN. "Preacher Dies with Heaven on His Lips" exclaimed the *Drudge Report*. Even Paul Harvey mentioned it: "Pastor Jack Arnold's last words were 'and when I go to heaven,'...and he went!'"

If my marriage had never changed, my thoughts during that ambulance ride to the hospital on that fateful day would have been very different. I would have been glad to see him go. While I certainly would have grieved the death of a human I knew intimately, a large part of me would have been happy to move on, my emotional side relieved.

How did I actually feel about it that day? I am happy to report that I was deeply saddened, grief stricken, and remorseful to lose my husband. By God's grace, we saw great healing in our marriage during our last two decades together. I had grown to truly love him.

<hr/>

I KNOW what some of you are thinking. You are disappointed that the story ends well. As long as I was struggling, you could identify with my situation. I understand, because I once had the same reaction when told that I could love my husband.

What was my response then? You don't know my husband! You don't know my circumstances. You don't know my lack of desire.

The purpose of this book, in large part, is to convince you that I do understand. I can relate. I know what it is like to be disgusted, to lose all desire for your mate, and to give up hope. To convince you, I have chosen to write a very honest portrayal of our marriage in the pages that follow. While some could interpret the candid details as embarrassing or even disrespectful to Jack and me, I believe the risk is well worth it. I have no doubt Jack would agree.

Mentors Needed

Love doesn't come naturally. And if it does comes naturally, it often goes away naturally. Many wives think about falling in love again with someone else after they are married. I had my first fantasy after three years of marriage, about the butcher at the A&P. I don't think I ever spoke to him, but I thought about him a lot, for about four months, then my feelings for him vanished, and I wondered, "What was that all about?"

Love is learned. It takes work. And you need mentors to get there. The Scriptures charge older women to "train the younger women to love their husbands" (Titus 2:4-5). We cannot do this alone. We need help and encouragement. We need coaching. We have the same needs that women had 2,000 years ago. Loving your husband is not a feeling. It is something you must be trained to do.

My prayer is that this book will help in that process. The first section of the book chronicles the story of my marriage, and I hope it will serve as a helpful example for overcoming the enemy of resentment. The second section provides thoughts and insights I have developed over the years. These insights are intended to help you understand your God-given ministry and empower you to avoid the ongoing temptation to resent your husband.

Women's Lib is So Yesterday

I want to assure you that I am not naive about progressive views regarding a woman's calling. I am the product of highly educated grandparents who held lectures in Los Angeles in the 1920s promoting free sex, abortion, and socialism. My parents were married for sixty-five years—lovely people who held very liberal, progressive ideas. They marched for whales, attended many environmental conferences around the globe, and were arrested for protesting nuclear weapons. At times they gave each other permission to have affairs, and encouraged the free expression of ideas and behavior.

So I am thoroughly acquainted with the world's message regarding what will liberate a woman. But I firmly believe that only a commitment to what God teaches in the Bible about the roles of husbands and wives will bring liberation to the sexes.

Seven Needs of the Husband

Much of this book focuses on the importance of understanding these roles, a crucial element of a successful marriage. But let me add that there are many important components of a successful marriage. My book discusses the wife's role at length, but every couple should also commit to other things that are extremely important. They include (1) submitting to the authority of Scripture, (2) committing yourselves to the local church, (3) allowing counselors and godly friends to examine your marriage, (4) and sacrificing your own desires for the sake of your spouse.

But wisdom and understanding are also very important. Proverbs 14:1 says: "The wise woman builds her house, but with her own hands the foolish one tears hers down." This doesn't say a *happy* woman, but a *wise* woman.

I believe a wise woman will understand that her husband has needs, that these needs are not sin, and that she has been perfectly created to meet those needs. It is very important for women to realize this, because if you look at your husband as sinful for being needy, you will not grasp the purpose of your calling as a woman. Instead, you will resent it.

One of the key turning points in our marriage was when I finally accepted the fact that it was good and right for me to meet my husband's needs. In fact, it was my calling and ministry, and I was specifically created to help this incomplete man who was simply the same kind of person that Eve found in the Garden of Eden, before sin had entered the picture.

Even in a perfect environment, with a perfect body and a perfect relationship with God Almighty, Adam was lacking. We read in Genesis 2:18, "The Lord God said, 'It is not good for the man to be alone. I will make a helper suitable for him.'"

After studying Genesis closely, I saw that Adam was created with seven specific needs that were met when God created Eve:

1. The need for *relationship*
2. The need for *authority and respect*
3. The need to *provide*
4. The need to *protect*
5. The need for *sexual fulfillment*
6. The need for *companionship*
7. The need for *domestic help*

Mothering My Six-Foot-Three Husband?

I believe that number seven, the need for domestic help, is perhaps the most resented need in our time. Think about what is implied here: Man has a need for "mothering."

Man's needs are met by his mother and father as he grows up. He is nurtured, cared for, loved, fed, and clothed by his parents. He is cared for when he is sick. He is encouraged to do well in school and told they are proud of him. When he is discouraged, they comfort and encourage him. They do all they can to make him the best person he can be.

When he marries, he is to leave his mother and father behind. Does his need for these things disappear? Do they go away now that he is married? No, they are still there, but many of them are now to be met by his wife.

Remember, these are the needs of perfect, sinless man, before the fall. These are needs created by God for the man to have as part of God's creation. How much more are the needs of our husbands.

So here we have the Creator's design for wives: to be a helper, to complement that which is incomplete without her. This is the biblical relationship that God created.

For years I resented my husband for having these needs. I refused to help Jack, ignoring my calling as a wife. While there were many layers to our recovery, the following pages will show you that my ability to overcome resentment was largely related to gaining a better understanding of my Creator's design for me.

Eve Deceived

I have also come to understand how easily I can be deceived, just like Eve was deceived in the garden. This deception leads to a corrupted idea of my helper design. Chapter 13 details how women so eagerly think they are doing something "good" when, in fact, our good intentions are like Eve's.

Another "Helper"

I never liked the word "helpmate"* to describe the woman. The term seemed subservient and demeaning, like a slave, like the kitchen help. But God impressed upon me one day that someone else in the Bible is called the helper.

Jesus said, "I am going to send you another Helper." This helper is the Holy Spirit, who is equal with the Father—truly God—but who has a unique and different role. This analogy between the Spirit and the woman is explored in Chapter 14.

The remaining chapters provide hints for married couples, advice for husbands, and a compilation of Bible verses to help you in your struggle to achieve a godly marriage.

AFTER RIDING in the ambulance to the hospital, I received the official word. Jack was dead. Thanks to the insights shared in this book—along with the help of supportive sons, close friends,

---

* "Helpmate" evolved from the old King James rendering of Genesis 2:20: "an help meet for him"—"meet" being an archaic word that means "suitable." Eventually, "help meet" became "helpmate" in colloquial usage.

gifted counselors, and many prayer warriors—my feelings and emotions that day were filled with love and compassion for my husband. I longed to be with Jack.

After many years of struggling as a pastor, Jack had turned a corner. He led a vibrant and growing church in Orlando and founded a ministry that sends teachers to train pastors in third world countries, especially Africa. This is a far cry from the depressed, hospitalized, perhaps suicidal man that you will read about in the following pages. I believe the fact God had changed my heart toward supporting and encouraging my husband rather than tearing him down was a major factor in the turnaround he made in his life.

Our new ministry had us traveling the world as husband and wife, working together regularly on meetings, mailings, and strategy sessions. We had become quite a team. When we taught together on marriage and the family, it was always a huge hit. We played cards together on the plane—usually cribbage or gin rummy—and we visited exotic beaches and ancient cities. We donned our African outfits and spoke to church groups. Back in Orlando we would go to the movies, go fishing together, and visit Sea World and Disney. At home I pulled the weeds while he planted flowers and cared for our two citrus trees.

I grew up with scores of pets and had always dreamed of going on safari. Jack's main boyhood memory of animals was being rushed to the hospital after two German shepherds bit him. Had you told me as a young pastor's wife that one day I would travel the world and regularly go on safari, I never would have believed it. I also never would have believed that my animal-fearing husband would be so excited to see the animals.

In our later years, Jack would talk with me over dinner about who to take next on safari. He wanted to make sure they saw all the big ones, he said, like the elephants and rhinos and lions. That might mean going to two different parks. He would talk about being the first to see a leopard in a tree, which is difficult to spot. He was so proud of that and mentioned it several times. We were having so much fun together, and we were enjoying new experiences. I did not want to think of life going on without him.

AGAIN, I KNOW that for some of you these positive stories are difficult to hear. But I want to assure you that it can happen for you as well. God did the impossible for me. He changed my heart, my emotions, and my desires, so that I loved my husband more at the end than at the beginning of our marriage (most of the time, anyway!).

The next section, the story of our marriage, starts with the beginning of our relationship. It did not take long for the challenges to emerge.

I know it is never easy. And just to show you that I have a sense of humor about it, I will end this chapter with a story I will never forget.

It was an easy three-hour drive from my home in Florida to the retreat center just outside of Palm Beach. I was the main speaker for a women's retreat with a group of over 100. As I pulled into the parking lot I noticed there were already quite a few cars, with more arriving. We were to meet for an early dinner, followed by some games, entertainment, singing, and my talk.

After checking into my room, I took a shower and changed clothes. Then I went to find the dining hall. Looking around the crowded room, I did not see anyone I knew, and no one approached me. I decided to see how long it would take before I was recognized as the main speaker.

I got my tray of food and proceeded to a table where a woman was already seated, eating alone. "May I join you?" I asked.

"Sure," she replied. "I'm new to the church, so I haven't met very many people."

I introduced myself, but she didn't recognize me as the speaker.

"Are you new to Florida?" I asked. Almost everyone is from another state, so this question usually sparks conversation.

"We were in Greenville, South Carolina," she told me.

"Oh, really? That's where we moved from also," I said. "What church did you go to? We were at Shannon Forest."

"We used to go to Shannon Forest," she said, "but we didn't like the preacher very much, so we left and went to another church."

"I didn't like the preacher very much then, either," I said. "But I was married to him, so I couldn't leave."

Part II

The Story of My Marriage

Carol Meets Jack

I HAD HEARD about Jack before I met him. He was a UCLA basketball player under Coach John Wooden. One of my sorority sisters had dated him and was very impressed because he took her on a picnic and read poetry to her (which he never did for me!).

I had also dated one of his fraternity brothers, but because I wasn't a Christian at that time, Jack didn't want anything to do with me. He had stated that he had been called to the ministry and planned to start seminary in the fall of 1957. To date a non-Christian girl was unthinkable.

I had just recently come to Christ during my sophomore year at UCLA, in February of 1957. I grew through the influence of several of my Gamma Phi Beta sorority sisters and also from the many activities that Campus Crusade for Christ sponsored for the students. I attended every meeting, study, and prayer service they held, as I had a new thirst for biblical truth.

Jack had a beautiful smile, pretty blue eyes, and was always neat and clean. He usually wore light blue, starched slacks and plaid, cotton shirts, often overlaid by a cardigan sweater or a letterman's sweater. He was a smart, straight-A student. (I secretly checked when I was working in the records department.) He was in one of the best fraternities, Phi Delta Theta, in which the top athletes and scholars were members. So he was a good student and a good athlete, but I was captivated by him mainly because I thought he was a godly man with a passion to serve and follow Christ. A lot of my friends respected him and knew him as a man who was very serious about his faith. And a couple of my sorority sisters had crushes on him, and so that also made him attractive.

At one of the Campus Crusade meetings in March, during Easter break, a small group met for prayer. We were asked to pray for Jack Arnold, because he had flown to Texas to give his girlfriend an engagement ring. So we prayed for him, for God's blessing on their relationship, for the parents' favor, and for safety in travel.

The week after spring break, Crusade held a large campus meeting. When the meeting ended, I saw Jack across the room. With my newfound Christian boldness, I went up to him and told him about my recent decision to follow Christ. He was very excited to hear it. Then I asked him about his trip to Texas and told him we had been praying for him. His face fell, his shoulders slumped, and his eyes teared up. "She dumped me!" he exclaimed.

He went on to tell me that when he got off the plane to meet her, she came up to him and said, "I've decided I don't want to marry you. In fact, I really don't want to see you anymore." When Jack asked her what he was supposed to do for the rest of the week, she told him he could take a bus to Houston and go stay with her parents, because she was going to remain in Austin and party.

He was so despondent and dejected that I couldn't help but feel sorry for him. I listened with genuine sympathy and compassion, and shortly he asked if I would like to go for coffee and talk. We went to a nearby Toddle House and talked until midnight (when I had to be back to the sorority house before lockout).

He was impressed with my desire to learn about the Bible, which I knew very little about. We planned to meet the next day after our third-period classes so he could give me some material to read, which he said would help me greatly. My third-period class was Home Economics, and we were baking cookies. I took some cookies with me to give to Jack (not knowing that cookies were his favorite food—after ice cream).

We continued to meet every day for the next three weeks, in the UCLA botanical gardens next to sorority row. It was a great place to be alone, to talk and pray without being disturbed. He helped me learn memory verses, gave me papers and sermons to read, and prayed with me. He seemed very knowledgeable about the Bible and was eager to share all he knew.

He told me how difficult the week was in Houston with his ex-girlfriend's parents. They had felt so sorry for him, and took him along to dinners and get-togethers with other old folks. They all loved having this tall, handsome basketball player at their parties, and every night he would have to answer their questions and tell them about his call to ministry. Their admiration of him was the only thing that helped him endure the otherwise dreadful week.

Jack also told me about his decision to go into ministry and that he was praying about whether to go to seminary in Princeton or Dallas. I would go with him when he would go to different churches around the city, teaching Sunday school and giving his testimony.

Meeting every day, getting together for coffee at night, and praying together at a nearby chapel . . . it didn't take long before I started to wonder if Jack was something more than a supportive brother in Christ. I loved being with him. He was good-looking and had such a desire to follow Christ. We talked by the hour about spiritual things and each other.

The more I was around him and saw his passion for spiritual things, the more I thought he might be the one I could follow to the ends of the earth, serving him and meeting his every need.

<hr />

I WASN'T at all experienced when it came to dating Christian guys, and I was wondering when Jack would try to kiss me. He didn't even try to hold my hand. I would dream about our first kiss, where it would be and how it would feel. It seemed like I waited a long time.

I remember the first time he reached for my hand and held it. We had just spent an hour in the chapel next to sorority row, praying and talking, and we were walking back to my sorority, which unfortunately was right next door. I could have kept walking hand in hand for a long time. Holding hands felt good—very good—and I was disappointed when he didn't try to kiss me good night.

Jack obviously wanted to honor God in our relationship, but the only way he has ever been able to control himself was by total abstinence. Whether it was alcohol (he was a strict teetotaler), eating desserts (it was either all or none, no moderation), or romance, he had to keep his distance. He once told me not to wear a certain sundress "because it's cut too low in front and causes me to lust!" I couldn't believe it and thought he was totally weird about such things, which I had never thought about before. But I admired his commitment to want to follow Christ and do the right thing.

One evening, as we were walking back to my dorm through the botanical gardens, he pulled me up to him and gave me a long and very sweet kiss. I was hooked. I would have stayed there for the rest of the night, but instead we slowly walked up the hill without talking. He was quiet until we reached the front porch. That's when he said, "You know, Carol, I'm thinking that maybe we should talk about marriage."

I thought, "Can't we just spend a little more time developing this romance thing before discussing serious issues?" But I told him then that I believed God was possibly showing me that he was the one for me—which was true. I just had never dated anyone so cautious before.

So for the next couple of weeks we prayed for God's leading and direction in our relationship. Jack wrote a friend who was in his last year of seminary to ask whether it would be better if he went to seminary married or single. I remember how hard it was waiting for that answer, wondering what he would say, knowing my future depended upon that letter. I looked up the word "wait" in a concordance, and was shocked to find 142 verses. I learned that waiting is very difficult, but is something that God often asks us to do.

After what seemed like an eternity, but was only three weeks, we received the reply: "Definitely come married if you feel you have found the right one!"

MY RELATIONSHIP with Christ began in February, I met Jack in March, we became engaged in April, and in May we planned an August wedding. In June we parted to go to our own homes for the summer.

Mine was in Guam, the tropical island in the South Pacific, where my father worked for the civil service. I traveled back to tell my parents that I had become a Christian, was quitting school, was getting married to a young man called to the ministry, and was moving to Dallas where he was going to attend seminary for four years.

My liberal, broad-minded, freethinking, existential, kind-hearted, hippie parents said, "Whatever makes you happy!"

That summer at home away from Jack was difficult. He would call me at night, when he missed me, all romantic and sentimental, but in Guam it would be one o'clock in the afternoon. It was always a bad telephone connection, and I would have to shout to be heard. He couldn't understand why I was so reserved when he was telling me how much he loved me, how much he missed me, and that he couldn't wait until August 20, when we would be man and wife. I would be in a room full of family, trying to keep my voice down, but Jack would keep saying, "What did you say?"

The time came when Jack wanted to take me to his home in Barstow, California, to introduce me to his parents. Jack was engaged twice before he met me and had a string of girlfriends before that, starting in elementary school. He was nervous about bringing another girl home to meet his family.

I got all dressed up in a new outfit for this special occasion. After driving for three hours, we arrived in Barstow, a small town in the Mojave Desert between Los Angeles and Las Vegas. Jack didn't want to just walk in the door with me and announce that this was the girl he was really going to marry—in just three months. So he said to me, "I'm going to drop you off at a park near my house. I'll go home, break the news to my folks about you, and then come back and pick you up." I thought this was a strange thing to do, but I agreed.

He took me to what looked like a vacant lot that had three or four picnic tables behind a fence and only a couple of trees. There was a cluster of teenage boys at one of the tables under a tree. I walked over to the closest table, which was in the sun, and sat down as I watched Jack slowly drive away.

The teen boys eyed me, laughing and talking to each other in Spanish. It was midday. The sun was blazing down. It was hot. I was nervous about meeting Jack's parents and about being alone in a strange park with a group of boys who had started moving to a table closer to me. Perspiration began to drip down my face, and I was worried that it might show under my arms.

After what seemed like hours, but was only minutes, I was relieved to see Jack drive up. He said, "I told my folks about you. But when they heard you were sitting in the park all alone they got mad, said I was crazy, and told me to come rescue you. So they may be in a bad mood!"

I questioned Jack's judgment at the time, but I thought, "I'll be able to help him after we are married."

CHAPTER 2

The Soil for Growing a Marriage

❦

I WASN'T RAISED in a Christian home. Growing up in California, my family never went to church. Sunday was the day we went to the beach or went camping in the desert or hiked up in the mountains. But strangely, I was the only one in the family whom God seemed to be drawing to Himself.

When I was in the fourth grade, a classmate invited me to a vacation Bible school run by Henrietta Mears at Hollywood Presbyterian Church. I had to memorize a strange verse—a man's name (John) followed by a number (3) and another number (16). I was told that if I learned it by heart I would get a prize, so I did. "For God so loved the world that He gave His only begotten Son, that whosoever believes in Him shall not perish but have eternal life." That was the first Bible verse I ever knew.

In 1947 my family moved to Guam, where my father became the chief design engineer for the Navy to rebuild the island after

World War II. While in junior high school, a friend asked me to sing in the choir with her at the Navy base chapel. I attended church regularly because I enjoyed singing. I couldn't tell you what the different chaplains preached on, but for the first time, going to church became a part of my life.

In the eleventh grade, I went back to California and lived with a friend to attend high school in the U.S. She invited me to her church youth group—a Presbyterian church. I didn't even know churches had youth groups. Again I was being exposed to the Bible, even though I don't remember anything I learned there.

I returned to Guam for my senior year of high school. One day my English teacher read something to us:

> Set me as a seal upon your heart,
>   as a seal upon your arm,
> for love is strong as death,
>   jealousy is fierce as the grave.
> Its flashes are flashes of fire,
>   a most vehement flame.
> Many waters cannot quench love,
>   neither can floods drown it.
> If a man offered for love
>   all the wealth of his house,
>   he would be utterly scorned.

She asked us if we knew who wrote these verses. We thought maybe Keats, Shelley, even Shakespeare?

"No," she said. "Let me read you something else from the same book." And she read:

> Love is patient and kind;
>   love is not jealous or boastful;
>   it is not arrogant or rude.

Love does not insist on its own way;
  it is not irritable or resentful;
  it does not rejoice at wrong,
  but rejoices in the right.
Love bears all things,
  believes all things,
  hopes all things,
  endures all things.
Love never ends.

I thought that was one of the most beautiful things I had ever heard! We still didn't know where it came from, and when she told us it was from Song of Solomon and 1 Corinthians in the Bible, we were all amazed. That thick black book with the small print that no one could understand? She said it was a new translation, in modern English, the Revised Standard Version.

I left school that day wanting to hear those words again, so I went to the library and checked that Bible out to take home. I read and reread those verses. I didn't believe it was God's Word, but as a young sixteen-year-old girl those verses had a strange and powerful effect on me. What I believed didn't matter. It *was* God's Word, and He was continuing to prepare and soften my heart.

For my high school graduation, an uncle gave me that version of the Bible as a gift. He didn't know I had been reading a library copy. It was the first Bible I ever owned.

I LEFT HOME to attend college at UCLA, and for the first time in my life I was lonely. I had left a school where I was a big fish in a little pond and was now at a school with over 25,000 students. I didn't know anyone there. I would go for days without ever seeing anyone on campus to say "hello" to. I had planned to join a sorority, but because I couldn't get a military flight out of Hawaii, I was delayed from attending Rush Week before classes began. (At that time there were no dormitories at UCLA, only sorority and fraternity houses.) I had to find an apartment.

I went to the Administration Building and looked up at this gigantic bulletin board full of names of people looking for roommates. That began a semester of weird and strange situations. One roommate didn't show up for three days, and I found out she was in jail for shoplifting. I changed to another apartment with three other girls and learned that they stayed up all night. Another set of roommates had gay friends for every meal, using up the food I had purchased.

I was very glad when I was able to go through Winter Rush and pledge Gamma Phi Beta Sorority. I moved into the sorority house and began enjoying the activities and camaraderie of living on campus.

One evening a sorority sister invited me to a large Christian gathering for fraternity and sorority members, hosted by Bill and Vonette Bright. They had started a new concept of reaching college students—future leaders—and had recently launched a ministry they called "Campus Crusade for Christ." Bill had been a successful businessman, but he had a zeal and fervor to reach the lost. He was young and full of enthusiasm, trying to look older by growing a mustache. One day he told me how excited he was because they had branched out to USC (the University of Southern California) across town and had a new staff member to help out on that campus. He said to me, "Carol, I envision in the future having Campus Crusade on all the major universities across America!" I remember thinking, "Yeah, right!" But I underestimated Bill and Vonette's faith, vision, and prayer life.

I wasn't interested in the message of Christianity, but everyone was so loving and friendly at those early Crusade meetings at UCLA that I kept returning. Also in those days, sorority pledges could not go out on school nights, except for "religious" meetings. So I went to all the Crusade meetings to avoid staying in and studying. Bible studies, prayer meetings, fellowships— I was at them all. I didn't believe anything that was being said, but I sure did enjoy the social scene. And truth was being taught, whether I believed it or not.

For over a year, I was a regular attendee at all the get-togethers that the Brights organized. Only my sorority sisters knew I wasn't a Christian.

At the main monthly meeting in February 1957, I heard the testimony of a young man who told about how God had provided the necessary money to stay in school after he had prayed about it. I thought, "Wow. That's nice. You ask God for something and then get it! Maybe someday I'll want that too—but not now."

At the end of the meeting, a new Campus Crusade staff worker drove a carload of girls back to their sororities. Gamma Phi Beta was the last house on sorority row, so I was the last girl to be dropped off. While I was in the car alone with the driver, he asked me, "Carol, how long have you been saved?" I answered, "I'm not a Christian!"

Well, for the better part of an hour he talked to me about what it meant to trust Christ as personal Savior and Lord of one's life. I remember asking him questions like, "What about the people in Africa who have never heard?" and "Why do you keep quoting the Bible? Why not another book? I don't believe the Bible." Several times I thought I would pray the prayer he was telling me to pray, just to get rid of him. But something kept telling me, "Don't do it. Don't be a fool. It isn't true. It would be a stupid thing to do. It's not what intelligent, scientific people believe. What would your family think?" I struggled for almost an hour, thinking of going ahead and praying, but something was holding me back.

Finally, I prayed the prayer for him out loud, "God, I don't even know if you are real. But if you are, and if you want to come into my life and change me and forgive me, go ahead!" At that moment, I knew I was a child of God, a "new creation in Christ," that the Bible was the Word of God, and that I had eternal life—and I've never doubted since that moment. It was years later before I learned about spiritual warfare and the fight that was going on for my soul.

Looking back I realize that the classmate who invited me to her vacation Bible school, the friend who got me to sing in the choir, the teen who took me to youth group, the teacher who read from the new Bible translation, even the uncle who gave me that Bible—none of them knew the significance of their actions and the overall impact they made in my life.

It wasn't until just a few years before my father's death that he told me about my first babysitter, Mrs. Thorbickson, a dear Swedish lady who had prayed for me, "lettle two-year-old Carol." I had no idea she had been praying for me. My father recognized her influence on my life. He said to me, "Your Christian faith might have started with her prayers!"

All of these people were part of the "tilling of the soil" to prepare me to finally receive the Word and accept it (Mark 4:20).

CHAPTER 3

Seeds of Resentment

EVEN THOUGH Jack and I had only known each other for three months before we planned to get married and I didn't know him well, I knew enough to know he would need changing once he became my husband.

I was like the bride who thinks to herself as she looks down the church aisle at her groom, standing at the altar: "'I'll alter him!" Every bride thinks her husband will change, and every groom thinks his bride will never change. That's a source of much frustration and conflict in marriage.

At times when we were dating, Jack had outbursts of anger, usually when he hadn't eaten, which were often directed at something insignificant. I once watched him pound the dashboard of his car because there was a rattle that wouldn't go away, and I remember thinking, "I'm sure he won't act this way once we're married. It's just sexual tension!"

One Saturday afternoon we were supposed to go for a walk together, but he called to say he was going to play an intramural baseball game with his fraternity instead. I thought, "Why would he rather play sports than be with me? That will certainly change when we get married."

❦

THE BEGINNING of our marriage was very shaky. Jack had a lot of crazy ideas, but I went along with his idiosyncrasies, convinced that I could not only cope with them but would be able to transform him into the perfect husband.

Take our wedding, for example. Jack said it would honor God to only have Christians at our wedding and that nonbelievers shouldn't attend. As a brand new believer, I didn't know any better, so I went along with him.

We were both from non-Christian homes, so that meant that none of our family members were invited to the wedding ceremony, which was basically an exchange of vows in the pastor's study. It was not so much a problem for me, as my folks were in Guam and one sister was in Japan, so it would have been very expensive for them all to come. But Jack's parents were deeply hurt, and it just added to the strain that was already there.

Jack invited two fraternity brothers to come. I invited one sorority sister, a cousin, and her boyfriend. The five of them stood behind us while the pastor recited the vows.

(Later Jack deeply regretted his decision regarding our wedding. He always encouraged the couples he married to have big weddings and invite everyone they could.)

❦

AFTER OUR five-day honeymoon, we spent a night at Jack's home in Barstow before driving halfway across the country to attend seminary in Dallas. His folks were still upset with Jack's decision to go to seminary instead of graduate school to become a coach. They had followed Jack's basketball career at UCLA with great enthusiasm, keeping all the articles about him, putting newspaper clippings in a scrapbook, telling all their friends about what Coach Wooden said about him, both very proud of it all.

So they were extremely disappointed after Jack became a Christian and decided to quit basketball and go into the ministry. Jack's father told him, "Son, if you go to graduate school to become a coach, I'll pay for it all, but if you go to seminary I won't give you one red dime." He was true to his word.

❧

My first flicker of resentment came during our first month of marriage. We had fixed the tiny porch into a study, with just enough room for a small desk, a chair, and bookshelves on the wall. Jack would read at his desk, so the light from his desk lamp wouldn't bother me. He was carrying a heavy class load his first semester at the seminary and would study late into the night, driven to make all A's. As I mentioned in Part I, when I would try to entice Jack to come to bed, wearing a skimpy nightgown, he would just ask me to make him another cup of tea. Once I gave him hot water with some food coloring in it, and he didn't notice that either.

Two months after the wedding I got pregnant. Not only had we not planned to have a baby, we didn't even think of it as a remote possibility. (The pill wasn't widely prescribed in the '50s, so family planning wasn't an exact science.) I had planned to work for four years to help put Jack through seminary. Instead we had four sons while in seminary.

With my first son, I continued to work until later in the pregnancy. Then I knew I would be working hard at the task of caring for a baby. My husband did not get a job.

To be fair to Jack, he was not being lazy but was redeeming the time and using every minute to study. The money that he would have made during extra study hours had been provided by a generous woman in Houston, Carolyn McManis. She was one of the ladies Jack spent the week talking to after his former fiancée left him in Texas. Several of the older widows there were smitten by him, especially Mrs. McManis, who was very impressed by Jack's commitment and zeal. (Providentially, he would have never met her if his fiancée had not dumped him.)

I had begun working for an orthopaedic surgeon as his only employee—secretary, office assistant, bookkeeper, X-ray technician, and receptionist—doing everything he didn't do. As the only other person in the office, I couldn't leave for even five minutes without going through the hassle of signing on the answering service. I worked every day from nine to five and every Saturday morning. The job was made harder by the unscrupulous activities of the doctor, including his practice of defrauding insurance companies by claiming patient treatments that he had never administered. When I would call it to his attention, he got angry and told me, "Just submit what I've written!"

Life was now a struggle. The long hours at a demanding job were emotionally draining, along with the uncertainty of the future with a baby. It was so hard to drag myself out of bed early each morning, struggling with morning sickness, a stressful job situation, and just plain weariness. Jack often didn't have classes until later in the day, so he would sleep in, having studied late the night before. I watched him snore, wishing I could crawl back into bed myself. But I had to go to work. It didn't take long before I was feeling overwhelmed, disillusioned, and bitter.

Jack was aware of this change in my attitude, but he was raised in a home where the father never helped with the housework (remember, this was 1957). I was feeling sorry for myself, working five and a half days a week. Saturday afternoon was when I took the dirty clothes to the laundromat, bought groceries for the week, cleaned the apartment, and ironed the cotton clothes we needed in hot, humid Texas. Many weeks would go by when all these chores weren't done. I remember pawing through the dirty laundry on Sunday morning, looking for a dress shirt that wasn't too badly soiled so I could iron it for Jack to wear to church.

As my resentment grew, Jack would say things like, "You're just out of fellowship. What you need is more time in the Word!" That didn't seem to help.

SOON JACK FELT the need to pray about the situation, as a good seminarian preparing for the ministry. He went out to sit in the car one evening after an argument. It was the only place to be alone, given our one-room apartment. God seemed to tell him to help me more, give me space and some time away, and provide me with opportunities to meet other women. He had heard about a Bible study for first-year seminary wives, but I thought I didn't have the energy to attend, and he didn't like the idea of having me take the car one evening a week when he might need it to go to the library to study. But he finally encouraged me go.

I joined five other wives, older and married longer than me. They were wiser and certainly more spiritually minded, as I had been a believer less than one year. We met in the home of a Scottish Presbyterian widow, Mrs. McPherson, who loved us, encouraged us, taught us, and gave us delicious desserts. The best time was the fellowship, when we shared our burdens, lack of money, and marriage problems. We prayed for one another, and it gave me the ability to cope during difficult days. We continued to meet for four years, and one friendship made there has lasted to this day.

Jack learned a valuable lesson as well. Women need other women. Men don't have the mind-set or ability to figure out everything about their wives. There are situations and problems that are only understood by other women. When Mary was pregnant with Jesus, she didn't confide only in Joseph, but sought out another woman—Elizabeth—to get the comfort and encouragement she needed.

❦

WHEN WE WERE first married, Jack and I communicated in totally different ways. We didn't know each other well enough to know what the other one really meant.

One evening, during our first year at seminary, I served fresh strawberries for dessert—splurging on this favorite fruit of mine when we had very little money. I gave part of the berries to Jack, and I had some. There were a few more left in the serving bowl, and Jack asked me if I wanted them. I said, "No, you go ahead and have them." So he did. He looked up and saw tears sliding down my cheeks. He said, "What's the matter?" I said, "I wanted some more strawberries too!" He said, "Well, you told me to go ahead and eat them!" I said, "Well, yes, but in my family, we would say to go ahead, and then the other person would say, 'No, you have them,' and we would go back and forth for awhile and then end up splitting them."

"Well," Jack said, "In my family we just told the truth."

❦

JACK DID VERY WELL in seminary. He studied hard and made good grades. He also taught a Sunday school class that everybody seemed to enjoy very much, and even at that time, while he was still in seminary, he handwrote, then typed, every detail of his teachings, word for word. Those written lessons (we refer to them as his "notes") were copied in the days when only mimeograph machines were available, and were then used in many Sunday school classes and Bible studies.

We had a lot of good friends and classmates in seminary who would come over to the house to discuss spiritual issues. I learned a lot of theology listening to their discussions while I quietly served coffee and cookies.

Fortunately for Jack I liked to cook, so we ate pretty well. I didn't learn until many years later that he needed food to keep from getting the jitters and becoming anxious, even angry, because of low blood sugar. I wish I had known his need for frequent nourishment earlier in our marriage. I would have kept at least crackers in my purse, and many arguments might have been averted.

ONE EVENING, about two weeks after seminary started, Jack left after dinner to go to the library to study.

"When will you be home?" I asked.

"The library closes at ten o'clock, so I'll be home soon after that," he replied.

I waited up for him to return. I expected him around ten-thirty. At eleven o'clock he hadn't come in. At eleven-thirty he was still out, and although I was tired, I waited up.

At midnight I started to wonder, "Where in the world is he?" I was angry. Then at twelve-thirty I started to worry. "We are new to the city," I thought to myself. "Only a few people know we are here. He only has his California driver's license. He isn't good at directions. Could he have gotten lost?"

Then I started to panic. "Oh dear! What if he had an accident and is in a hospital somewhere? Maybe he's unconscious! He doesn't have anything on him to let them know he is married, where we live, or how to get in touch with me!"

As the minutes ticked by, I decided to call the police. Just as I picked up the phone, I heard the car pull into the driveway.

When he walked in the door, he was surprised to see me. "You're still up!"

"Where on earth have you been?" I wailed through tears of anger and relief.

"Oh," he replied. "I met a bunch of guys in the library, and we went over to the Toddle House for coffee. We were just talking theology for awhile!"

From that night on, whenever Jack was out late studying at the library or anywhere else, I thought, "You might be unconscious in a ditch somewhere, but Buddy, you'll never have me to worry about you again."

CHAPTER 4

Kids and Complications

WHEN THE TIME came closer to deliver Mark, our first baby, I was convinced that it wouldn't be very hard to have natural childbirth. I didn't know about Lamaze classes or have any inkling of how to care for a baby. My mother had said she would come to Dallas from California to help out, but we said, "No, we can manage by ourselves."

The night before Mark was born we had strawberries for dessert—and this time I had eaten a lot of them. So many, in fact, that when I started having pains around two in the morning, I thought it was a stomachache from having eaten too many strawberries. After several hours it became clear, however, that this was more than too many berries. I tell you this to show just how ignorant I was about pregnancy, labor, childbirth, and babies.

After a long and grueling labor—alone, as no husbands were allowed in those days—I gave birth to a nine-pound two-ounce baby boy. I needed an episiotomy, forceps, and two blood transfusions, so I was not in great shape. Yet when Jack came in to visit me, he complained about not having enough sleep because he had to wait in the lounge until the delivery.

The next day we brought baby Mark home from the hospital to an empty house with dishes still in the sink and with an overwhelming sense of "What now?" Jack said to me, "I know you don't want to cook supper, so I'll just go out to eat." And he drove off! I sat down in the rocking chair, this new infant in my arms, my body hurting, my stomach hungry, and my heart aching. All I could think was, "What about me?" The resentment grew.

That night I called my mother, and she took the first available flight to Dallas.

My mother had been a pediatric nurse as a young woman. Her father was a family doctor. She gave me encouragement, support, and tips on motherhood that helped me the rest of my life. Even to this day, teaching on parenting as I travel around the world, I often give advice my mother gave me.

***

ONE OF OUR main struggles was the constant lack of money. Jack said he couldn't take a night job, like many of the other students, because he didn't come from a Christian home and had a lot of catching up to do. We had a new baby, and it was our conviction that I should stay home to take care of him and not leave him at a day care while I worked. So we had only a little money coming in from the McManis fund.

To supplement this meager income and help with the rising expenses of a new baby, I started typing papers, theses, and dissertations for the seminary students. I got twenty-five cents a page, which I thought was big money. In those precomputer, pre-Xerox days, even before electric typewriters, all pages had to be typed without one error on the page, using two carbon papers and margin liners behind the first sheet.

I remember one evening, typing the same page over and over again, making a mistake near the bottom of the page, ripping them all out of the machine and starting over. After nine or ten attempts to finish the page without one error, I was in tears, with crumpled paper all over the floor. Jack came in from the library, saw the sad state I was in, gave me a hug, and told me to quit for the evening, get a good night's sleep, and start fresh the next day. It worked. The next morning I completed the entire paper with only a few pages that needed retyping.

I typed many papers for the students, and learned a lot of theology in the process. I typed for Charlie Swindoll and Hal Lindsey, the other two students supported by Mrs. McManis. Hal figured out that my typing skills were accompanied by cooking skills, as he came over almost every day for coffee and my homemade chocolate chip cookies.

One Sunday morning we found ourselves without milk for the baby, only a tiny amount of gasoline in the car, and just a few coins in the entire apartment. Jack was scheduled to teach a Sunday School class that day for a large church, and as he drove off with barely enough gas to get there, we assumed they would provide a "love offering" for teaching the class, knowing he was a poor seminary student.

After the class, many people came up to him and thanked him for the good teaching, but no one gave him any money.

He was discouraged and confused, knowing he would run out of gas on the way home and arrive without milk for baby Mark. In his frustration he went outside and walked down the block, having thirty minutes or so before the church service began.

This church was only two blocks from the seminary, and as he walked closer to the campus, something said to him, "Go check your school mailbox."

He dismissed the thought, because he had checked his box late the night before, and no one worked in the school on Sunday morning.

But he had the urging again, "Go check your box."

He thought that it would be a waste of time, even silly. But the urging continued, so he made his way across the campus, down the steps to the mail room, and opened the combination lock, all the while feeling foolish. To his surprise, inside the box were two one-dollar bills: one for gas, one for milk.

To this day, those two dollars remain one of God's greatest provisions in our lives.

***

I HAVE NEVER been very time conscious. I rarely wear a watch and keep time by the sun more than the clock. Jack, on the other hand (a German, type A, choleric), was a stickler for time and wanted to account for every minute. He was never late and thought tardiness was an abomination.

He once said to me, "Hurry up! We're already twenty minutes late." And we were on our way to an all-day church picnic to relax and play.

I showed up fifty minutes late for our wedding ceremony. I remember thinking, "Just relax, don't rush or you'll get perspiration on your dress." When I arrived at the church Jack was furious—and embarrassed in front of his friends. He said to me, "Carol, how could you be so late? I'm not sure I want to go through with this!" The pastor appeared, saw Jack's angry red face, and asked, "Is anything wrong?"

I replied (as I always did during conflict), "No, everything is just fine!"

My tardiness was a source of many strains and conflicts throughout our marriage. I made Jack late to dinners, parties, meetings, and church services. I thought I would be able to change Jack's obsession with being on time, but I never did. He changed me, however, for which I am grateful. I realized how insensitive, even selfish I was all those years to keep Jack and others waiting.

✦ ✦ ✦

WE LEFT DALLAS after five years of seminary and after Jack's first year of study toward his doctorate, to begin a church plant in central California. We had one car and lived five miles from the church, and I thought, "How in the world am I going to get myself, Jack, and three (soon four) little boys to church on time, dressed, fed, and in fellowship!"

It took a concerted effort, starting on Saturday night, but we did it.

Jack's job every Saturday night was to shine all the shoes. (Those were the days of leather oxfords for boys.) Sunday morning he was to dress the boys with the clothes that I had laid out the night before, while I fixed him a big breakfast and put dinner in the oven. I don't remember ever being late to church after that. It's amazing what a little planning and preparation can do to make life easier.

✦ ✦ ✦

JACK HAD a very soft conscience. He agonized when he was convicted of a wrongdoing. He had difficulty keeping a secret and a hard time hiding feelings of guilt.

When he was a first-year seminary student, he looked at a classmate's paper during a test and changed his answer. That evening his guilty conscience forced him to confess to me that he had cheated. He tried to call the professor to tell him, but he was out of town. All weekend he was in anguish because of his transgression. I thought he was being irrational. On Monday morning, he drove to the seminary, even though he didn't have any classes that day, and went to see the professor.

He told the professor, "I want you to give me an F on the test because I cheated on one answer. I feel so badly and tried to reach you, but you were gone."

The professor said, "You obviously have been punished already by having to think about it all weekend, so I won't change your grade." Then the professor added, "Oh, by the way, your original answer would have been right."

I first learned of Jack's ultrasensitive conscience before we were married. We were at a picnic sponsored by a campus church, at Griffith Park, about an hour away from UCLA. Jack had been talking to a couple in the church and mentioned that a mutual friend had been guilty in the past of cheating on his wife.

When we got back to the campus, Jack felt very sorry that he had gossiped and possibly even been wrong. He decided to drive all the way back to the park, find the couple, and apologize to them. I told him that was absurd, to spend the next two hours or more tracking them down. "Just call them tomorrow," I said. But he said he had to go. So he drove all the way back, looked around the park until he found them, and apologized. Their response? "We don't remember the conversation we had with you."

JACK WAS a strong teacher. He taught several times a week while still in seminary. Even then he loved mentoring and discipling the younger men. He received the Loraine Chafer Award for Systematic Theology, which was the highest award given to theology majors. And he loved preparing his lessons and putting them into note form so others could learn from them.

We had anticipated working with Campus Crusade when we finished seminary, so I never thought I would be a pastor's wife. However, an incident during Jack's first year in the doctoral program changed his ministry direction.

We had a young single man over for dinner, as we often did. He had been on staff at Crusade and planned to return after graduation. Jack showed him a set of notes he had just completed, which had taken a lot of time and study.

He looked at the notes briefly and said, "Jack, why do you want to waste your time doing this kind of stuff when you can go out and win the world for Christ!"

I watched as Jack's face fell with disappointment and hurt. Later he said to me, "I want to study, teach, and preach. I guess Crusade isn't the place for me." (Much later we learned that we would have fit just fine with Crusade, and that this young man was asked to leave the organization for moral failure.)

God used that painful event to direct us into the pastorate, which previously we never would have considered.

WHEN IT CAME time to find a church, after Jack received his doctorate in theology, he candidated at several places that made me quite nervous: very cold places, very hot places, too small towns, very large cities. He finally reduced the list to four churches: one in Texas, one in Michigan, his first choice in Newport Beach, California, and his last choice, Roanoke, Virginia.

Jack waited for the search committees to extend him a call. Grace Church in Roanoke wrote right away, asking him to come, but he kept waiting to hear from the other churches. He waited until he couldn't put it off any longer. He told Grace Church, "I'll let you know in three weeks." He assumed that in three weeks he would hear from these other places, but he didn't. So he took the position at Grace Church. We thought,

"We've never lived east of the Mississippi River before. Maybe this will be an interesting experience, and in two or three years we'll move back to California."

The week after he arrived in Roanoke, he received letters from all three of the other churches, asking him to come. But by then he was committed to Grace Church, where we stayed for over sixteen years.

When Jack arrived at Grace Church, it was a small group of people from various theological persuasions and backgrounds. The church had been started in the early '50s by a group of Presbyterians who had left the mainline denomination, which was too liberal for them. They didn't have a denomination to join, so they started Grace Presbyterian Church, Independent. Before Jack came, they had a pastor who was Baptist, so he changed the name to Grace Church, Independent. When Jack came, he dropped the word "Independent." Some of the members were afraid that soon the name would just be "Church."

<hr/>

JACK BEGAN to teach, and slowly the church evolved into one of the more prominent churches in the entire Roanoke Valley. When organizations like InterVarsity, Campus Crusade, Child Evangelism Fellowship, Christian Women's Club, Young Life, or Navigators were looking for leadership and committed people, they knew they could find them at Grace Church.

Jack was well respected in the community. He was on the radio. He began a school, Grace Academy, which was considered one of the leading Christian schools in the area. He led the building of a large sanctuary, with a balcony and rooms above and a full basement with classrooms and library below. Then came an administration building, also two story, with additional classroom space. The church budget was never in the red—always in the black—and the missions budget went from $12,000 when he arrived to nearly $80,000 when he left. All of this was accomplished with a congregation of less than 400 people.

Through all these years of good and positive ministry, when Jack was a much-beloved pastor, I was secretly harboring animosity and guilt, because I didn't love Jack the way I knew I should, the way I thought all other wives felt. I was going through the motions of being a good wife, but my heart was cold and unaffectionate.

My resentment continued to grow as Jack seemed to get needier in our marriage instead of becoming more self-sufficient. I felt that he took me for granted, and that all the things I did for him were simply expected, without considering what I wanted to do. Clothes were washed and ironed, food was purchased, three meals a day were prepared and served, the house was cleaned (sort of), and little boys were cared for, day in and day out.

CHAPTER 5

Dr. Jack and
Mr. Hyde

❧

ALTHOUGH THIS may be true for many spouses, it was definitely my experience and feeling that Jack could be sometimes admirable, sometimes terrible. The following stories demonstrate the challenges of marriage when your spouse appears both good and bad, like two creatures in the same body.

⟨⟨⟨⟨⟨⟩⟩⟩⟩⟩

IN THE EARLY '70s, several black couples visited the church. It absolutely horrified some of the southerners but thrilled Jack. One wealthy elder threatened to leave the church and used the "n" word. Jack told him, "Don't you ever use that word again in my presence, and if you want to leave the church, there's the door!" And he left. Jack assumed he was the biggest giver in the

THE LIBERATION OF A RESENTFUL WIFE

church, and it caused him to panic. But right after he left, we got a flood of new people. Jack made it a policy not to know who gave what in the church and discovered later by happenstance that this wealthy man didn't give all that much to the church anyway.

The first black couple was Charles and Kay James. They came to Christ in college through InterVarsity, and wanted a good Bible-teaching church. They had tried all the black churches in town, then someone told them about Grace Church. It was a risky move to attend an all-white church, but they had a very strong desire for biblical and theologically sound teaching. It wasn't all smooth sailing, but Charles became a deacon in the church, and all the black couples who followed had a positive impact on our congregation. Our son Mark, who was in the middle of his rebellious period, thought it was so cool to have them there. The Jameses even kept Mark in their home for a week when Jack and I had to leave town.

Charles's business took him to Richmond, however, which led to Kay (Coles) James becoming spokesperson for National Right to Life and later a member of George Bush, Sr.'s cabinet.

Another couple was Willie and Kathy Boone. Willie, later known as Wellington, attributes the saving of his marriage to Jack's counseling. Since then Wellington has been a keynote speaker for Promise Keepers and has spoken to some of the largest Christian gatherings in American history.

◆━━━━◆

It was an exciting event for me when our youngest son, Dean, went off to all-day school for the first time. It meant that all four boys would not get home until after two-thirty in the afternoon. During Dean's first week at school, I went to a Bible study in the home of Phyllis, one of the most hospitable women in our church. After the study, she invited several of us to stay for lunch.

DR. JACK AND MR. HYDE

I readily accepted, feeling a freedom from having to pick up a child at the church nursery or at half-day kindergarten.

We were all in the big kitchen, chatting and helping prepare some sandwiches. I was really enjoying the fellowship and conversation. The phone rang, and Phyl said, "Carol, it's for you. It's Jack."

I took the phone, wondering what he wanted. "Hello."

"Carol, I came home for lunch. Why aren't you here fixing it?" he demanded.

I was flabbergasted! I held my hand over the phone and told Phyl what Jack said. "Have him join us for lunch too," she replied.

"Honey," I said, "I'm having lunch with some of the women at the Bible study. Phyl said for you to come on over and join us."

"No, I don't want to have lunch with a bunch of women! Come home now and fix my lunch here."

I refrained from slamming the phone down, told the women I had to go, and rushed out before they could see the hot tears swelling in my eyes. My anger, and my nerve, mounted as I drove the short distance home. When I walked in the door, I went up to my waiting husband.

"Don't you ever, ever call me again and make me come home to prepare your lunch. I've waited years for the freedom to stay gone during the day, and I don't want to have you at home demanding lunch! Fix your own lunch!" I ran upstairs and slammed the bedroom door.

Later Jack came in and apologized, after he had eaten the sandwich he fixed himself. He never again called me home for lunch. I just bought more jars of peanut butter and jelly.

THE MORE RESENTFUL I became as a wife, the more I looked for opportunities to minister outside the home.

I started speaking at Christian Women's Club luncheons when the boys were in junior high. When they organized the first club in Roanoke, they came to our church to find women to lead it. They got the maximum number that was allowed from any one church, and it wasn't too many years later that they asked me to be a speaker. I would travel to various communities around Virginia, North Carolina, South Carolina, West Virginia, and Maryland. I would give my testimony about how I became a Christian or some stories about my kids. I didn't speak so much on marriage then, because I knew in my heart that my marriage wasn't doing too well, even though I was fooling everybody but me and God.

I would drive on Thursday morning to speak to working women that evening, then give the same talk at luncheons on Friday and Saturday. The meetings were usually at hotels or country clubs, with about 300 women attending. I did this two or three times a year, and enjoyed getting away from home and meeting new people.

LIKE THE INCIDENT with the black couples, our congregation was tested again when a large group of young people walked into church one morning and sat down in the front row. Sporting bare feet and long hair and wearing T-shirts, they were what was then called "Jesus freaks." Their leader was 17-year-old Richard Pratt, now a well-known author and professor at Reformed Theological Seminary. They had previously been attending a "coffee house" church, but had heard about Jack and wanted to see whether they would be accepted.

Again many of the people were horrified, but Richard tells the story: "After the service, we went up to Jack to talk to him and ask him questions. He took his coat and tie off, pulled off his shoes, sat down on the carpet, and spent over an hour talking to us and answering our questions. I will never forget it."

They realized that Jack was a man they could trust and learn from. The following year Jack performed (and I directed) about thirteen weddings for many of these kids who were getting married. Richard and Gena were one of those couples.

Jack's premarital counseling was considered the "best in the business," and at his wedding ceremonies he "tied a very tight knot," as one father remarked. Jack performed over ninety-five weddings in his life, and could count only about six divorces. I was a wedding director, by default, because no one else knew what to do. I heard over and over the vows that were being taken, and it had an impact on me as I considered my vows as well, even though I wanted to break them.

Jack would not marry couples who were engaged in premarital sex. If they were active, he would tell them to back off for three months and that then he would consider marrying them. One couple came to him three months later, and when Jack asked if they had refrained from sex, the girl said they had. Her boyfriend spoke up, "Janet, what are you saying? We haven't backed off, and you can't lie to Jack!" Jack said, "The counseling session is over. You can find a justice of the peace to marry you. I have had scores of couples that have met my standards, and I cannot lower them for you." Janet called him a dinosaur and left.

ONE MORNING Jack and I were arguing over who would get to use our only car that day. I was convinced I needed it to go to a Bible study. Jack said he needed it to buy some books that were necessary for his sermon preparation.

As he started out the door to take the two younger boys to junior high school, I blocked his way and said, "I'll take them to school."

He said, "No, I'm taking the car," and he shoved me out of his way with his elbow.

Being the manipulative drama queen, I stepped backward and allowed myself to fall, hitting the lamp on a table, which crashed to the floor, with me on top of it. Jack stormed out the door and left.

I got up, unhurt but miffed that my tactics had not worked, and sat down with a welcomed second cup of coffee.

Several moments later Jack appeared at the door.

He said, "I'm so sorry to have shoved you. I was wrong to get angry. Please forgive me."

He was very repentant and asked me what he could do for the boys who witnessed it, to make things better.

I asked David and Dean about this years later, as I had forgotten the details of the incident. They said they were sitting in class at school when Jack appeared at the door. They looked up and saw him and were surprised. He walked over to each of them and said, 'Son, come with me. You're leaving class.' Then they went home, packed a few things, and spent the next two days together on Smith Mountain Lake, fishing, talking, and relaxing.

⁕

THERE WAS a young schoolteacher in our church who wanted more than anything to find a good husband. Jim was her best friend, a really nice guy, and they enjoyed being together and going out, but she was not interested in him at all romantically. She kept praying that God would bring her a husband, and she would often go to Jack for counseling, telling him that she liked teaching school but really wanted to be married. Jack would counsel her and encourage her to keep praying about it. All the while, she and Jim would hang out together.

One day she came to Jack and said, "Guess what? Jim is dating Rose!" She continued, "I'm angry and hurt. I'm having these funny feelings like jealousy, because he's my friend and he's dating Rose! Do you think it might be that Jim is really the one I want? Do you think I'm really in love with Jim?" Jack said to her, "Well, Betty, you're not a teenager anymore. If that's the way you feel, then you'd better go to Jim and tell him and let him know. You're a grown woman; don't play games!" She went to Jim and told him her feelings. Four months later they were married. Now they have five kids.

Another young woman had a similar conversation with Jack about wanting to find a husband. She was a pretty girl but had a bad case of acne. Jack said to her, "Have you ever thought about going to a dermatologist?" She was horribly offended and said, "I've been to the doctor." He said, "Well, go to the dermatologist." She left, offended and hurt. But she did follow his advice. In two months her face cleared up, and five months later she was married to one of the young doctors in the church.

<hr>

WE DID A LOT of entertaining in our ministry, both in our home and in the church. Jack loved parties, enjoyed having people over, and loved being the host. We often had "Game Night" and invited a number of couples.

Jack's favorite game was the "Cities Game." I would cut pictures out of magazines to provide clues that corresponded to the name of a city (like a picture of holly and a picture of some wood, which would signify Hollywood). He would hold up the clue and say, "Now what do you see here? What is in the picture?" Jack loved to lead that game, even though he had a terrible time remembering the cities. He would help me get ready for the games and then help me clean up afterward, because he enjoyed having them so much.

Even back in seminary he loved to have people over, but we were so poor it was impossible to feed a group. So we would have potluck suppers and invite some of our more well-to-do friends. They would come with all this wonderful food, and then whatever was left, they would let us keep. We were able to eat for about a week on the leftovers.

Jack had a very big social side, enjoyed people with a quick wit, and was an easy target for ridicule and pranks. He was often the brunt of jokes—the fall guy—and people loved to make fun of him. Jack would laugh and enjoy the jokes on him, most of the time. (Even at his memorial service there were many "Jack stories." As Richard Pratt commented in the closing eulogy, "I've never been to a memorial service where they roasted the deceased!")

But when I would ridicule Jack in public, it was often cruel. He would tell me later, "That hurt me, what you said." And I would reply, "I was only kidding!" I later came to realize that this was an excuse to be hurtful and mean.

CHAPTER 6

*It's All About
the Kids*

❧

WHEN MARK started junior high, Jack was enmeshed in the church, and I started getting involved in school activities. We started spending a lot of time away from each other.

I became president of the PTA several times and attended state conferences. I worked a lot with the band director and traveled to performances and parades as a chaperone. When our second son, Brian, moved to high school, I became band booster president, and the trips became longer as we traveled to Louisville, Orlando, Niagara Falls, and Washington, D.C. I spent even more time away raising money; working on uniforms, flags, and banners; and planning meetings.

Then I joined the board of Young Life and became a camp counselor, traveling by bus to Windy Gap and Frontier Ranch in Colorado. It was all great fun, and I saw a lot of my son's friends, as well as my youngest son, Dean, come to Christ through this ministry. However, the more I became involved in these activities, the more I neglected Jack.

I was grateful to Jack for his desire to work with his sons in sports and that he spent many hours coaching football and basketball. That was one thing I appreciated. But when it came to music, school activities, or even Young Life, he wasn't interested. The more I got involved with those things, the more Jack withdrew from family life, because the conversations with the boys revolved around Young Life and band.

The high school made students choose either band or sports. When our third son, David (now known as Arny), chose band over basketball in high school, Jack was hurt and disappointed. He was very proud of their musical accomplishments, especially the swing band they were in, because Jack loved the "big band sound." His father had played clarinet in his own swing band back in the '30s, and Brian now played that same clarinet. But Arny's choice made Jack sad, because he believed Arny had extraordinary athletic ability.

<hr />

DURING THIS SEASON of our life, the kids started having their friends over to the house a lot. Our house was where the kids would show up and hang out. Friday nights or whenever, if there was activity, it usually was at the Arnolds.

I would go with one of the boys to the public library to rent old reel-to-reel movies before the days of DVDs and VCRs. We borrowed the church projector and showed the movies on the white wall in our living room. Charlie Chaplin, Hitchcock, even National Geographic—the kids really didn't care what they watched as long as there was a place to hang out. I would make popcorn and the kids would bring beverages. I must have popped hundreds of gallons of popcorn. Then we would sit around after the movie and talk—often late into the night—and I would watch Jack quietly creep upstairs and go to bed, alone.

I ALWAYS WONDERED why all the teenagers wanted to come to our house, because Jack would sometimes yell at them and tell them to go home. "Get out of here," he would tell them. "You've been here long enough." I'd ask them why they liked to come to our house when Jack yelled at them. They'd say, " 'Cause we know that if he's not yelling, then we're welcome." They'd go on to say, "Many homes we go to, nobody says a word to us, but we can tell by their cold silence that they really wish we weren't there. But we feel welcome in your home until Jack says something, then we go home."

Many of those kids were from broken homes, and they appreciated having a man in the house. One young boy later told Jack that he used to long for those days in the church when Jack would give him a hug and rough up his hair a little bit. He also said that sometimes when he was over visiting our house and Jack would have to spank one of the boys, he wanted to say, "Spank me too. I deserve it too."

JACK WAS a good disciplinarian, but because I was from a family of all girls, I thought his discipline was too harsh. Spanking was rare growing up in my house. Our boys seemed to need spankings often. And there were times I tried to prevent them from being disciplined, even when I knew they deserved it. Later I came to appreciate the strict but fair discipline Jack meted out.

Jack had spanking guidelines. He spanked on bare bottoms only. He spanked with a belt or switch. He only gave three strikes. If the boys ran away, fought, or wailed, they would get one more switch. He never used his hand, as the Bible says to use "a rod." The hand is meant for blessing.

Because we had all boys, we tended to treat them all alike, which was a mistake. They are very different, and in looking back, I wish we had recognized that. They were pretty rowdy at home, but we never had any problem with babysitters. They were always well behaved in public and with other people.

JACK WAS WORKING himself to death, taking on more and more ministry opportunities. He was preaching every Sunday morning and every Sunday night, preaching Wednesday nights, teaching a Sunday school class, speaking on the radio once a week, and leading a home Bible study.

He was also teaching seminary-level classes at the Roanoke Institute of Biblical Studies (RIBS), which he originated in our church. Several pastors would teach two nights a week for forty to fifty serious students of the Bible who would come from all around the area. They would get certificates for completing a semester-long class. Jack usually taught a class on theology. He was also on a TV panel discussion group once a month. He spent many hours studying, writing, and typing up the notes for all these different talks and lectures.

The busy schedule started to wear him down, but he loved teaching and was driven to work as hard as he could.

I WAS BUSY TOO, teaching at the women's Bible study at our church. I also began teaching a study for about twenty women in Rocky Mount, twenty miles south of Roanoke.

During this time I would get up very early and go downstairs before anybody else was up. I'd fix a cup of coffee and go to a big chair in our den where I kept my Bible and two pencils (a yellow one and one with red on one end and blue on the other). I would read at least a chapter every day, going through the whole Bible, underlining as I read: red for promises, blue for warnings and admonitions, and yellow for verses on prayer. It was an incentive for me, because I was very proud of the fact that there wasn't one chapter in my Bible that didn't have something underlined in it.

Then I was taught by somebody that you could take a black pen and outline a letter in such a way that it made the words bigger on the page. So I started doing that. I spent an awful lot of time underlining and making words bigger and not so much time paying attention to the things I was reading. My motivation wasn't to have my heart changed as much as it was to gain knowledge—and to get that underlining done.

At times, I would go up the hill and jog two or three times around the big church parking lot. Thinking I was sound in body and spirit, I would go home and face the day—a day that often would include being unkind much of the time to my husband, even though I may have just been reading about mercy, forgiveness, and grace.

CHAPTER 7

Depression and Breakdown

THE CHURCH was growing quickly and was full of activity. Jack had a large staff but needed an associate to help preach and teach. He hired a good friend whom he had known through RIBS and the Sovereign Grace Theological Society. It was a mistake, however, because even though Jack loved him dearly, he and Jack were going in two different directions.

Because Jack was so busy and tired, he was not able to handle the conflicts, which slowly caused him to slip into depression. The more depressed he became, the less he was able to lead the church in the direction he wanted it to go. When he realized he was losing control, he was not capable of exerting leadership, and people started leaving the church.

The direction of the church became more and more formal, more solemn. The music changed. Nothing but traditional hymns could be sung on Sunday morning; the more informal hymns "in the back of the book" were reserved for Sunday night.

The teaching even changed, as Jack alternated preaching every Sunday with the associate pastor. The associate remarked one Sunday that it bothered him to hear laughter in the parking lot after church, that people were not being introspective about his messages if they could make jokes after the service. Many of the people who left the church told Jack later that they thought it was Jack who wanted the changes, and they just couldn't take it anymore, it was too depressing.

It ended with the church splitting and Jack in depression, having to be hospitalized and on medication.

<hr />

JACK WOULD come home and become more and more withdrawn, to the point where pretty soon he wasn't able to do much of anything. He would often just sit in a chair and maybe watch TV. And he would start crying and weeping. This would happen a couple of times a week, and then it got so that he wasn't able to interact with us at all.

The more involved I became in the lives of my children, the more withdrawn Jack became. The more Jack withdrew, the more I escaped into my children's activities and adventures. This vicious cycle continued for most of the boys' adolescent years.

Band, drama, basketball, Young Life—my boys were involved in all these things. The kids were such fun. At home we would be up in the living room playing games, sitting around the piano jamming, playing music, or telling stories about what was going on in all our activities. Jack would be downstairs in the den, watching television, completely out of it, no fun to be around at all. Therefore Jack was not only at home in depression, but he was home *alone* in depression. I realized that he needed some help, but I thought time would take care of it.

◆━━━━◆

JACK AND I took a trip to Rehoboth Beach with our friends Bob and Sunny. I thought it would be a great time for Jack to wake up and "snap out of it." That was my way of comforting him.

Bob tells the story of going to get donuts one morning while we were at the beach. In the car Jack turned to him and said, "Bob, I don't know if I'm a saved man. I have my doubts." His depression had caused him to lose his grip on God as well as life in general.

That afternoon we had a time of prayer together for about an hour. Jack never opened his mouth.

A few weeks later, it was time for Arny and Dean to return to Covenant College. I packed up the car and got everything ready to go. Before they pulled out of the driveway, I asked Jack to pray. He said, "Well, let's pray. Lord, we want to thank you for this food..." Then he stopped and said to me, "Carol, you'd better pray." It was then I realized that something was terribly wrong and we needed help.

I don't remember whether I took him to David, our psychologist/counselor friend in the church, but David sent him directly to another doctor in the church, a neurosurgeon. When he examined Jack he said, "Jack, you are in clinical depression, and I am putting you in the hospital because you need treatment. You need to be watched, and we need to monitor you to see what we can do to get you help."

I was stunned. I knew Jack was depressed and discouraged over the church situation, but I thought if he stopped worrying about it, thought about the positive things, and "looked on the bright side," everything would be okay. David had said to me,

"Carol, you are like the friend in the school yard when a bully comes and socks your buddy in the stomach and then runs away. You're telling your friend, 'It's okay now. The bully is gone. Nothing to worry about.' But your friend is doubled over in pain, and you're not letting him catch his breath. Jack is in pain, he needs time to heal and get over the blow, and you're not giving him what he needs."

Jack had described me as being like one of "Job's miserable comforters," but now I realized I really was being mean and cruel to someone who desperately needed compassion, care, and love.

I remember visiting him in the hospital and still thinking to myself, "You should snap out of this. You have a choice to be happy or not. You have the choice to be depressed or not." So when they said to me, "Jack will have to take medicine to get him out of depression." I thought, "Well that's a bunch of baloney, but if it helps him get out of this gloom-and-doom attitude, it's fine with me."

When he returned home two weeks later, he still wasn't in very good shape. He wanted to sleep all day and do nothing. I remember dragging him out of bed one afternoon. "Let's go buy you a new fishing pole," I said, thinking that would raise his spirits. He went, but he was just going through the motions.

Jack was so out of it, yet I had little compassion on him all during this time. I felt like he was getting his "just desserts." He thought too highly of himself, and that's what he gets.

I believed Jack to be a very proud man. He did have a lot to be proud about, I'll grant you that. He did well in school and seminary. He won the Chafer Award for the outstanding theology major. He received praise for his doctoral dissertation, "The Pauline Doctrine of Progressive Sanctification" (on how to live the Christian life). His church was strong and healthy, without money problems. He was tall, good-looking, and distinguished.

But I thought he was overly prideful. I heard him say on several occasions, "What's a guy like me, with a doctor's degree, doing in a small church in a small town?"

I believed it was part of my mission to destroy Jack's pride. I didn't want to say or do anything that would encourage him to feel proud of himself. Therefore I took every opportunity to shame or humiliate him, both in private and in public.

He was getting very little encouragement or support and very few strokes from me during all this. Oh, he got three square meals a day and clean clothes, but he was not getting the "I'm proud of you" kind of response from me. No encouragement. No empathy. No sympathy or any of those things. No "mothering" that encourages a loved one to cope with difficult times or helps them overcome their sadness. I wasn't doing any of that. I was in the "snap out of it" mode.

JACK TOLD ME later that in the midst of his depression, God spoke to him and said, "Because of your pride, you're going to eat grass like Nebuchadnezzar for seven years." He answered, "No, Lord, no." God said, "Because of your pride, Jack, you're going to eat grass for seven years." I didn't know that had happened or I probably would have left him right then and there.

About this time, when our last son left for Covenant College and we had an empty nest, Jack made the decision to leave Grace Church. This is when I had the hardest time controlling my resentment and bitterness. I was leaving Grace Church and Roanoke, my home for over sixteen years. I loved the people in our church and the city of Roanoke. I thought I would grow old there. I was involved in the community. I had even thought about running for the school board.

A year earlier, Jack had joined the Presbyterian Church in American (PCA) through the influence of Dominic Aquila, one of the pastors who had attended the Sovereign Grace Theological Society meetings in our church and had stayed in our home. But Jack was still pastoring an independent church and felt it was time to lead a church in the denomination and was asked to start a new PCA work by a group of people in North Carolina. My only consolation in leaving Roanoke was that we were moving just two and a half hours away, to Kernersville. I knew I could drive up periodically to visit my friends and the church, which gave me comfort.

It was still very difficult, however, and when the movers had everything packed into the truck, ready to pull out of the driveway, I went upstairs to use the bathroom. When I stood at the sink and realized I would never again look into this mirror, I burst into tears. I was angry at Jack for taking me away from my comfortable home and into a new and unfamiliar part of the country, a new group of people, even a new denomination.

Kernersville was a nice town, nestled in the foothills of the Blue Ridge Mountains, and it served as a bedroom community halfway between Greensboro and Winston-Salem. We found a nice ranch house to rent on two acres, with three bedrooms, a large living room, and a huge above-ground swimming pool in the backyard. The landlord was happy to rent it to us at a good price because we didn't have kids or pets and we didn't smoke. Also, his college-age daughter wanted to continue to live in the mother-in-law apartment in the back, which was fine with us. Our furniture fit nicely, we settled in, and I started to enjoy the area.

We had high hopes and tremendous expectations. Our vision was to develop a ministry center that would involve lots of different activities. The man who had invited Jack to Kernersville said he had talked to the presbytery and had a group of millionaires to support the work. We were renting, with the option to buy, an old college campus that had an auditorium, classrooms, dormitories, a gymnasium, and a dining hall. It was run down and needed renovation, but we thought it would be a tremendous opportunity, and we both got very excited. We even brought some of the Grace Church people down to visit the campus.

We had our first church service at the Holiday Inn. About 100 people showed up. Because they had advertised that Jack was a graduate of Dallas Theological Seminary, most of the people were from a Baptist or independent background. We then started meeting on the campus, but it was summer, it was hot, and we had no air-conditioning. We used fans, but it was humid and miserable, and a lot of the people couldn't take the heat. We just kept thinking how nice it would be in the fall.

But after six weeks, the group that called us dissolved, the leaders didn't get along with each other, and the man who had invited Jack to come resented it when the others started looking to Jack as their pastor. We discovered that what we thought would be a PCA-sanctioned church plant was never planned by the presbytery, and that there were no millionaires in the group. Jack was left without a call, a church, or a salary.

There were a few couples that came faithfully to the services and enjoyed Jack's preaching. But we didn't have enough money to pay the rent, so when everything fell apart, we continued to meet in our home, setting up chairs in the large living room and using a spare bedroom as a nursery.

For nine months this small group of twenty to twenty-five people came every Sunday. One young man played the piano, another the guitar. We took turns taking care of the little children. Jack preached. The offering paid the rent, with a little extra to help with groceries and utilities.

But it was very difficult to leave a successful ministry and come to this. We were at the lowest point in our marriage: no kids, no money, no church, no fun. Jack and I were together 24-7. His study was one of the bedrooms, so he was there all day long—a first for me. We couldn't go anywhere because we couldn't even scrape enough money together to go to the movies. I didn't know anybody. The kids were all gone. It was me, Jack, and the four walls.

It was a dark home: wood paneling in the dining room, floor-to-ceiling bookshelves in the bedroom we used as Jack's study. I spent most of my time in the kitchen and in our bedroom, alone.

I was disappointed that everything had gone wrong. I was angry that we had left Grace Church. I was disillusioned about our situation. I was fearful about what the future might hold. Jack was miserable and felt like a failure, and was no fun to sit across from at the dining room table. He slipped back into depression and later said to me, "I wanted to end it all. But I didn't know what to use, a knife or a gun."

CHAPTER 8

Friends

AFTER A COUPLE of months, I was so miserable I decided I couldn't stay one more day. I took some grocery money, put gas in the car, and drove to Roanoke to escape to my friend Sunny and to get away from Jack, Kernersville, and my life there.

For several days I poured out my heart and told Sunny how wretched my life was, how terrible my marriage had become, what a difficult place we were in, how the people had deceived us into thinking there was a church starting up, and how we had no money and three kids in college.

Sunny listened, patiently let me rant and rave, loved me, and cared for me. Then she said, "Carol, I've listened and heard what you've had to say. You've been here long enough. Now it's time for you to go home and be a good wife."

"I don't want to!" I pleaded. "Can't I stay?"

"No, Carol. You need to do the right thing. And the right thing is to be a good wife to Jack, who needs you now more than ever."

I knew it was true, but I didn't want to hear it.

Nevertheless, I drove home. On the way, through the beautiful Blue Ridge Mountains, I prayed and cried. I begged God to help me get out of this mess, whatever or however that would be. I knew I couldn't continue the way things had been. We were not helping each other, and we certainly were not helping to build the kingdom of God. It was during that two-hour drive that the Holy Spirit gave me the strength to pray, "God, help me to make things better—for me, for Jack, and for the church."

A few days after I returned home, I called a job placement agency and got a temporary position as a secretary for a group of psychologists at a large children's orphanage. Although I hadn't worked for over twenty-five years, it was a good decision. It got me out of the house for most of the day and enabled us to have a little more money. Meanwhile, Jack continued to pursue a pastorate.

***

IT WAS a glorious day when Jack finally got a call to a wonderful church in Greenville, South Carolina: Shannon Forest Presbyterian. Again I was skeptical about leaving, but it was only three more hours down the road, so I knew I could drive back to Roanoke without too much trouble.

Jack and I prepared to leave Kernersville. We packed up the house and his books (47 boxes) and sold some old furniture. The people came and gave us a farewell party, and promised to write. (To this day there are people from that tiny group who support our ministry, Equipping Pastors International.)

We arrived in Greenville, again with high hopes and expectations. This was Jack's first Presbyterian church, and he was very excited. He started a series of messages called "A New Beginning." Unfortunately, the church didn't want a new beginning. They were mourning the loss of their beloved pastor, who had started the church twenty-three years earlier and had only recently left town. I don't think there was a man on earth who could have walked into that position and been received with open arms.

Jack said there wasn't one session meeting that didn't include the implication that Jack wasn't the right man for the job. He would return home looking like a whipped puppy with his tail between his legs.

On the other hand, I was enjoying the church. I helped organize a women's Bible study, which I taught. I helped my gourmet cook friend Sally prepare delicious homemade meals every Wednesday night for the church, which caused the attendance at prayer meetings to quadruple. I loved opening my home to the friends my kids would bring home from college. I especially loved getting to know Jan, a student at Covenant College, who later became a daughter-in-law. For me, life in the church was good.

A LOT OF the parents had kids in college, and we would get together on Sunday nights after church and meet at Cracker Barrel for fellowship. Whoever wanted to join us was welcome. Pretty soon we realized we were spending too much money eating out, so we started meeting in different homes every Sunday, each couple bringing their leftovers from Sunday dinner. We called it "the Group." We all had such fun together, remembering birthdays and anniversaries, telling about what was going on with our kids and in the church.

That fellowship was like a support group for me. It was a good time of fun and fellowship that included Jack. Those friendships sustained me, so that even though I was struggling in my marriage, I was not struggling as much in my overall situation. I loved the people in the church, I liked my home and neighborhood, and I liked the city of Greenville.

So when Jack came home early from a session meeting and said he was fired, I couldn't believe it. I was devastated. I then did something quite out of character for me. I got in the car and immediately drove over to the church where the elders were still meeting. I walked into that room filled with men and told them they were making a terrible mistake. I actually fought for my husband for the first time in my marriage. I was mad, hurt, angry, and crying. Later some of those elders told me how much they appreciated that I had stood up for Jack.

Why did I do it? One reason is that in Greenville I had made a commitment, a mental commitment, to stay in my marriage. I wasn't so sure at Kernersville. There I wanted to flee, but in the back of my mind I knew I couldn't, even though I had been toying with it a little bit even before Kernersville, in Roanoke.

I was thinking, "I don't know if I can live like this for the rest of my life. I just don't know if I can live with someone I don't love. It's so *hard.*" But in Greenville I had begun to think—in a subtle way, and not even obvious to me—that I was in this marriage for the long haul. Jack and I together were able to cultivate friendships that sustained me. I found he was a sociable man whom other people liked and respected. Even though I didn't think I could admire him, I noticed that other people did. The people in "the Group" loved him, and so I thought, "Well, there is something there for them to love, even if I don't see it that much."

BUT THINGS were still awful for our marriage in Greenville. One night Jack and I were in our bedroom, and I was already in bed, reading. When Jack got into bed, he turned off the light. I said, "Excuse me, I am reading!"

"Well, you know I can't sleep with the light on," he replied. I turned on the small lamp next to my side of the bed, which barely gave me enough light to read. Jack said, "Turn the light off!"

"It's barely shining on my book—there's no way it could be keeping you from going to sleep. You sleep in the middle of the day, on the sofa, in your chair, even in the car! You mean to tell me this little light is bothering you?"

He reached over to turn my lamp off, and I grabbed his hand and pulled back on his finger. He yelped in pain.

"I'm not going to walk on eggshells around you anymore," I said. "I'm tired of it. I just can't live like that any longer, and I don't want to live in fear when you don't get your way."

Jack said later that I became a little more feisty in our marriage. I told him, "Well, my life got easier." He said, "Well, mine didn't."

I had come to the point where I had lost so much respect for Jack that I really didn't care anymore what he thought of me or how he thought I felt about him. I just decided I wasn't going to make him the priority of my life. I was going to do my own thing and pour my life into my kids.

CHAPTER 9

Breakthrough in the Rockies

THE SESSION of Shannon Forest knew we were struggling, not just because of the church situation, but also in our marriage. So as part of Jack's severance package, they wisely included a two-week visit to Marble Retreat, a counseling center for couples in ministry. At first I was skeptical about going, not knowing what to expect, but then I looked forward to the opportunity to go because I still was thinking that Jack was the one who really needed help. I wanted our marriage to last, like all women who, given the choice, want lasting, happy marriages. Like me, they just don't think the marriage they are in can be happy.

Marble Retreat is nestled on the side of a mountain in the Rockies, a four- or five-hour drive from Denver. Even though it was June, there were snowcapped mountains all around.

Next to the retreat center is the trout-filled Crystal River, which cascades over rocks and boulders. The lodge is rustic, made with stones and logs, but very beautiful, with a large stone fireplace to take the chill off the evening mountain air. Cozy chairs in the den and games in the recreation room provide comfortable places where you can occupy your time. There is a small dining room where delicious gourmet meals are served for the guests. Upstairs are four guest rooms, spacious and well appointed, each with a balcony that overlooks the pine forest and offers a magnificent view of the mountain peaks in the distance.

Marble Retreat was started by Louis and Melissa McBirney, who both previously worked at Mayo Clinic. She was a psychologist and he a psychiatrist. Together they had seen among the clergy so many illnesses and medical problems that stemmed from difficulties in ministry that they had the vision to start a counseling center just for troubled pastors and wives.

Jack and I were one of four couples—the maximum allowed —and we had an interesting group. One pastor was a missionary who put on women's clothes every time he was discouraged. Another pastor from New York was there with his wife, who had repeatedly cheated on him, but they wanted to save their marriage. The third pastor was an Episcopalian priest from California. He was very quiet, thin, and small. His wife was twice his size, very loud and domineering. He was afraid to open his mouth in front of her. They had one son who had changed his name from David to "Star Zephyr" and had joined an occult group. Then there was Jack and me.

The first session with the McBirneys included all four couples. They explained the rules: Over the next two weeks we would meet as a group twice a day, several days a week. We were free to ask anyone in the room any question we wanted, and we were also free to reply, "I don't want to answer" to any question we were asked.

During the first two or three sessions, different ones started asking Jack questions, mainly because he was willing to answer any questions they asked. Then they started nailing Jack about how they thought he seemed arrogant and proud, and how they didn't like his know-it-all attitude. I just sat there thinking, "Right on! Right on! Keep it up!"

He walked out of those first sessions shaken and visibly upset. "I don't know if I can go back to that room," he said. "I just can't take it."

<hr />

SEVERAL TIMES a week we would meet as a couple, and then we would also meet individually with a counselor. Meals were served to the whole group, which gave us time to get to know each other in a more relaxing atmosphere.

We were given a lot of free time with which we could enjoy ourselves alone or with other couples. Several of us went horseback riding. Jack and I did a lot of fishing together for trout in the river, which we brought to the chef, who expertly prepared them for all the guests. We walked up to the marble quarry nearby and explored a little ghost town a half mile up the river. One day several of us drove to a nearby snowcapped mountain where we hiked up to the snow line. Another day we drove into Aspen to take in a summer concert on the lawn.

All these activities were fun, many were new experiences, and Jack and I enjoyed being together. When we were alone, we would talk about the other couples and their problems. We didn't know that there were people in ministry whose lives were so screwed up. They started making us look healthier.

However, when we would meet as a couple, we didn't seem to be getting to where we needed to go. At the end of the first week, I still felt that I was fine, but that my lot in life was to put up with a miserable husband. I just said, "Well, I'm fine, I'm happy."

⬥

As we became more and more familiar with the other people in our group, they started opening up to us, sharing their feelings and problems. Interestingly enough, Jack and I actually had a tremendous ministry with the couple from New York and the missionary couple. It was significant to me that Jack had such a positive influence in their lives. We even exchanged Christmas cards with them for several years. The Episcopalian couple from California, however, seemed beyond help.

During the second week, they started zeroing in on me and my problems. I was astonished to learn that they thought I might be part of the problem in our marriage.

At one of the individual counseling sessions, Louis asked me, "Carol, I've been watching you. Why do you always have to be right?"

"What do you mean?" I answered, completely taken aback by the question.

"I've observed that when Jack is telling a story you often interrupt and correct him. No one cares if something happened on a Tuesday instead of a Wednesday."

I was miffed, but didn't say anything. "Choose your battles," he said. "Many differences in marriage are trivial and not worth fighting or arguing over." He continued, "What is more important, you being right or Jack's dignity?"

I was astounded. It was true! I corrected Jack publicly all the time, and never cared about his dignity or self-esteem.

The next night we were with Louis and several other couples, waiting to go into the dining room. Jack was telling the group about something that had happened that day, and I corrected him on some inconsequential point. Louis turned to me and said, "Carol, you're doing it again!" Then he turned to the group and said, "One of the best lessons I can give you is to teach you to say, 'So what.' In light of eternity, does it matter? Actually, will it matter the next day?"

All of us realized how many of our disagreements and arguments fell into the "so what" category. From then on I tried to catch myself wanting to correct Jack, struggling with the need to "always be right." Even though I often failed, it made for a much happier relationship.

<hr>

ONE OF THE BOOKS the McBirneys gave us to read was *Talking Straight* by Ron Adler. It was a thick paperback, and I didn't read it completely through. But I read enough to get the gist of it. Couples often argue because they don't say what they are feeling. Instead, they mask their true feelings by talking about how they want the other partner to act a certain way.

An incident that happened during the second week at the lodge helped me to see this principle in action and learn from it. There was a table in the den with an unfinished jigsaw puzzle set up on it. I love all kinds of puzzles—especially jigsaw puzzles—but I rarely had the luxury of sitting down and putting one together (except on New Year's Day, while Jack spent the day watching football). This particular puzzle was a beautiful landscape of the spectacular Colorado mountains with a rocky stream in the foreground. Jack and I had been fishing at such a place a few days before, early one morning, and had caught seven trout, which we brought back for the cook to fry up for breakfast. The puzzle picture reminded me of that spot.

One evening we were all sitting in the lounge having coffee and chatting. A couple of us were working on the puzzle. Then everyone said good night and went up to bed, including Jack. I stayed downstairs, looking forward to working on the puzzle by myself.

A short while later, Jack appeared at the top of the stairs and whispered, "Aren't you coming to bed?"

I said, "No, I'm not in the least bit sleepy. I'll come up after awhile."

He then said, "We have to get up early tomorrow for a breakfast meeting."

I replied, "I know. I don't need as much sleep as you, so you go ahead."

"You'll bother the others," he said.

"They're already sound asleep," I answered.

Now I know what some of you are thinking—Jack wanted Carol to go to bed with him so they could "snuggle" (as Jack would call it). But that had happened that afternoon, so I knew that wasn't Jack's motive for wanting me to go to bed with him.

I asked him why he cared if I stayed up late anyway. And his reply was a tremendous eye-opener for me. He said, "I feel neglected when you are working a jigsaw puzzle!"

He was "talking straight," telling me that his true emotion was a feeling of neglect. His other reasoning I could argue with, but I couldn't argue about the feeling of neglect he was experiencing. I realized then that many of our disagreements were because one of us wasn't telling the other what was really on our mind and what we were honestly feeling.

CHAPTER 10

Insights

No DOUBT the greatest lesson I learned at Marble Retreat was from a tape I was given to listen to about husbands. I don't remember much about the tape or who was speaking—I wish I did. But I remember one point that changed my attitude about Jack.

It was about the difference between pride and ego and how important it was for the wife to build up her husband's ego.

It said that the ego is what makes a man feel like a man, and when he is shown respect and admiration, it causes him to feel good about himself, builds his self-esteem, and makes him a better husband. I had always equated ego with pride. I didn't want to build up Jack's ego, because I thought he was very prideful and I needed to break his pride. I didn't want to do anything to make him more proud, so I didn't compliment him or build him up.

I learned that it is God's business to break one's pride, not mine, and that a wise wife is going to build up her husband (Proverbs 14:1).

About this time is when I came to the place where I said to God, "Oops, I need some changes in my life. I'm partly to blame for the difficulties in our marriage. I guess I can't point my finger at Jack as the only one who's the problem here." I said to God, "I need you to start working in my life."

That's when it seemed like the Scripture just started opening up to me, and God began revealing things to me about my own life that were very profound. He helped me recognize that I was on the right track, and that He was blessing my desire to be obedient. He assured me that what I was doing was moving in the right direction according to His will for my life.

<hr/>

THE HOLY SPIRIT was teaching me these things in little bits and pieces, not all at once. But I started recognizing the needs Jack had, and that they were not sins, but rather a lack of completeness placed there by God. And I began to understand that my ministry was to be the one who would complete and complement him.

I "knew" these things, but it is one thing to know truth and another thing to apply it. I've told you I had spent all those hours in the Word, reading the text and underlining verses. Someone said, "It's not how many times you've been through the Word, but how many times the Word has been through you." As I read the Bible with these new convictions, the words began to touch my life, and I found myself saying, "Wow, this is what I was created to do. This is a neat thing. This is God's will for my life. This is how things are, and I haven't been listening to God. I've been listening to the world and the flesh and the devil!"

It wasn't good for Jack to be alone, and I had been leaving him alone a lot. He didn't do well alone, and God revealed to me that this was something I needed to understand. It wasn't a weakness on his part—it was the way God had made him.

Then God began to give me other insights. That Jack was to be my provider and protector. That he had the need for sexual fulfillment, which only I could give him without causing him to sin. That he had the need for companionship and "mothering." That he had the need for respect, and that I had been bent on destroying his ego—his self-esteem, his manhood. It breaks my heart to think how cruel I had been to him.

As I learned from God about these needs, I realized how far short I had fallen in understanding *my* ministry—the ministry of marriage.

You see, all along I thought Jack was so needy because he was such a sinner, and I just resented it, terribly resented being the one to meet the needs of a sinful man. It didn't seem right.

It was a big turning point in my marriage when God revealed to me that although Jack had many needs, these needs were not sin. In fact, they were put there by God Himself. And He created me with the ability and design to meet those needs.

All of a sudden, instead of being resentful, I realized I had been given a challenge by God, a challenge that might be difficult, but not more than I could bear. Many people have ministries that are difficult; some are far more difficult than others. But most women are capable of meeting challenges when they understand that these challenges are given by God, and for God, as a ministry.

❧❧❧

I'M GRATEFUL for the lessons learned at Marble Retreat, although at times they were painful. I've learned that growth only comes through trials and tribulations. "A calm sea never made a skillful mariner." I've never heard anyone say that they grew during days of ease and comfort.

When we returned from Marble Retreat, I wasn't a completely new woman or wife, but I knew that I was on the right track and that my attitude toward Jack had changed. Our next place of ministry helped even more.

When Jack left Shannon Forest, they gave him a generous severance package that allowed us to take our time looking for our next place of ministry. One church that was very interested in Jack was in Winnipeg, Canada.

We flew up there in April—in fact, it was the weekend of the Masters Golf Tournament in Augusta, Georgia, not far from our home in Greenville. It's always a joy to watch, with the azaleas in bloom and the beautiful landscaped fairways. When we arrived in Winnipeg, I didn't see one blade of green grass or one flower anywhere. It was cold, flat, and ugly.

Jack seemed to like the church and the opportunity he would have to teach at the Winnipeg Bible College nearby. It was a large church—old established families with considerable wealth. We stayed in an elder's home, a lovely place, and the hostess was polite but rather distant and cool, I thought. On Saturday morning we were to look around the city at houses and get a feel for the area. It began to snow. I wasn't prepared for such weather, coming from the beautiful springtime in South Carolina. I asked my hostess if I could borrow some gloves or mittens, because I hadn't brought any. She said, "I think mine would be too small for you."

I started to think about how far away we were from our family and friends. Winnipeg is 250 miles north of Minnesota and the U.S.–Canadian border—pretty much out in the middle of nowhere. I thought, "I'll never see anyone I know again!"

The more Jack had positive feelings about the place, the more panicked I felt. I didn't like cold weather, I didn't like big churches, and I certainly didn't like the thought of living so far away from every single person I knew on earth.

That night in bed I began to pray and ask God to forgive me for what I was going to have to do. I had determined that the next day I would act so ugly that they wouldn't want to hire Jack because of his mean wife. I pleaded with God to forgive me for doing it, but I knew I couldn't move to such a place.

After about twenty-five minutes of agonizing prayer, asking God to forgive me ahead of time for my actions, it was as though He reached down, patted me on the arm, and said, "There, there, Carol, don't worry. You and Jack are not coming to Winnipeg!"

"Oh, thank you, God! I'm so relieved!" I remember saying. And I fell asleep.

The following Sunday evening after church there was a meeting of all the church leaders to talk with Jack. The main people in control were the church secretary, the choir director, and the director of children's ministries—all older single women. They didn't seem to get along very well with Jack. Normally I cringe when there are strained relationships, but that night I just sat there and smiled. We didn't go to Winnipeg.

No, indeed. Instead God directed us to Orlando, Florida— where the Canadians go for vacations. It was a marvelous move for us, and the end of the seven years of God's discipline.

The church God called us to was small but full of delightful people. When Jack came home from the first session meeting, I was a little anxious, because in the past those meetings had been so painful. But he walked in the door smiling. I asked him how the meeting went. He replied, "Well, after the first thirty minutes I had to ask the men to get serious." I knew we were at the right place.

NOT LONG AFTER we got to Orlando, I was asked by the church to teach a Sunday school class to women. They wanted me to teach on marriage. A lot of my new understanding evolved out of that class because I was actually trying to apply what I was studying, and our marriage had started getting better. I even called the class "Redeeming Your Marriage," even though I still had a long way to go in my relationship with Jack.

But through that study and through the desire to be a better wife, I started learning more and more about God's pattern for marriage. I didn't yet have the concept of companionship, or "mothering." These came later as I studied and taught. But God was giving me the opportunity to think through the ministry of marriage and how it looked in my life.

I never had an older woman sit down with me and talk to me about these things. Titus 2:5 says that older women need to teach younger women how to love their husbands, because it doesn't come naturally (and what does come naturally often goes away naturally). The wisdom that comes with age and experience is needed to give younger women the ability to look down the road and work toward what all women around the world really want: strong marriages and healthy families.

When I travel to Africa or India or Brazil, women are the same regarding their desire for a successful marriage and their struggle to make it happen. Almost every woman I've ever met has come to the place in her marriage where she realizes that what she thought was love is not there anymore. The world is teaching us that love is this feeling of romance and passion, and as older women we have to teach the younger women that this is only a small part of what love is.

Love is commitment. Love is having a vision, being wise, recognizing and understanding a goal for which you can sacrifice the moment, because something more important is down the road. Love is working to attain that goal, which is a marriage that not only glorifies God but also *lasts*, so that your children and grandchildren can see that you persevered in honoring and keeping the vows you made at the beginning of your marriage.

Marriage is also a picture of the relationship between Christ and the church (Ephesians 5:32), which is a tremendous goal to show the world. It is an honorable and good thing, and we need to applaud marriage and recognize that God instituted it as the first and most basic foundation of society. People like Oprah Winfrey are saying things like, "You don't need to get married. Why do we need marriage? Let's have committed relationships, but we don't need marriage." These ideas are permeating our society. But we do need marriage, because it's a picture of Christ and the church.

Think for a minute about what this really means—a picture of Christ and the church. The Old Testament is filled with pictures of how God made a way for people to come back to Him after our fall into sin.

The first five books of the Bible describe an elaborate system of offerings, sacrifices, priests, the tabernacle, the ark of covenant, etc. All of these are pictures of how to restore fellowship with God.

The historical and prophetic books of the Old Testament are filled with accounts of how God was calling His people back to fellowship with Him, reminding them to be faithful to the pictures He had given to them.

But right there at the very beginning, in Genesis, was the first picture, a picture of love and fellowship and unity and intimate relationship, the picture of marriage. From the very beginning, marriage was meant to illustrate the kind of relationship God wants to have with us.

Christ came to fulfill the Old Testament pictures, which all pointed to Him and His work on the cross. This includes the picture of marriage. All of us who know Him are called his "bride," and we will join Him someday at the marriage supper of the Lamb.

So why do we need marriage? It is a picture to the world of the most important relationship of all.

CHAPTER 11

Mickey Mouse

MOVING TO ORLANDO was a huge benchmark in our marriage, because for the first time in many years, Jack and I started having fun together, just the two of us. One of the first things we did after getting settled was buy season passes to Disney World. We would go down to see a show, or one attraction, or just walk around and enjoy the sights.

Each time we went it made us a little closer, and the experience of doing things together strengthened our relationship and caused us to enjoy being together. I've often told people, "Mickey Mouse saved my marriage."

Probably the biggest change in me was that I never said no to Jack when he wanted sex. In the past I had tried to avoid it in a hundred million different ways, like most women do. I even avoided hugging him (even though I longed to be hugged), because I knew where it would lead. But part of understanding my ministry of marriage was to meet his needs for sexual fulfillment. Even though it might not have been a good time, I didn't say no. I said, "Not now." That way I wasn't rejecting him, but letting him know that there would be a time for us to be together later.

Whether it was cooking meals, washing clothes, letting him get more insurance, or finding ways to compliment him and let him know I appreciated the things he did for me, it all became a joyful ministry. I knew that when I took care of Jack and met his needs, I was doing God's will. The center of God's will is a wonderful place to be.

What was even more wonderful was that the more I took care of Jack, the better husband he became. A man with needs isn't a complete man, and for years Jack had been like a cripple, unable to reach his potential, because he needs weren't being met. He wanted me under his thumb. He was often harsh and angry. He got frustrated with his ministry and with life in general.

I witnessed a dramatic change in him as I tried to be a better wife. He started helping me more. He brought me flowers and gifts. He was a better husband, a better father, and a better pastor. He gave me more freedom, and I had more opportunities to travel and develop ministries around the country—and soon around the world.

The woman in Proverbs 31 is certainly liberated and free. She's a businesswoman, she travels, she manages a successful home and also works in the community. She does crafts and has small businesses as well as real estate. But her secret is found in the first two verses written about her: "The heart of her husband trusts in her…she does him good and not evil all the days of her life" (NASB). Her first priority is her husband and making sure his needs are all met. Then God lavishes abundant opportunities upon her. I've experienced that same lavish abundance.

⚜

NOW THAT I look back at the way I treated Jack, it breaks my heart. It was awful, what I made him go through. But in God's providence, it made him a better pastor, because later in life he counseled scores of pastors who were in depression. He recognized it and was able to tell them, "You need treatment, you need medicine, and you can't get yourself out of this on your own." I've had many men, after he died, call me on the phone and tell me, "I'm back in the ministry today because of Jack's encouragement and counseling."

Some of them were repentant men who had had indiscretions, some of them were men who were in depression, some of them were men who had conflicts in their churches—and they all said, "Jack was the only one who would shoot straight with me."

I even had men call me after Jack died and say, "I need Jack right now. I've got a situation in my church and I don't know of anybody else in the world who could have helped me but Jack. I miss him right now." I had another pastor call me who said, "I've got a situation going on that's going to require me to put on my 'Jack hat'!"

When Jack came down to Orlando and joined the Central Florida Presbytery, he was one of the oldest men in the presbytery. Early on they asked him to serve on the Minister and His Work Committee, the committee that handles the pastors' personal problems. Although the normal tenure is two years, Jack was asked to chair the committee year after year. He had a tremendous impact in that ministry, but I do not believe it would have happened without my commitment to meeting his needs properly.

❦

AFTER TEN YEARS in Orlando, our church gave Jack a sabbatical. He wanted to spend part of it overseas, so he contacted a friend with Campus Crusade for Christ and asked if there were any teaching opportunities in another country. He was told they needed an adjunct professor to teach in Kenya, at the Nairobi International School of Theology, so we went. We spent a month there—two weeks teaching and two weeks visiting my sister, an artist who is quite well known in Kenya, where she has lived for over forty years. It was a wonderful experience, and we fell in love with the people. Jack's classes included students from eleven African nations.

When Jack returned to the church, he couldn't get the faces of those students out of his mind. They were so hungry and eager to learn, more so than the students at the other seminaries where Jack had taught throughout the U.S.

After several months, Jack approached his session and asked if he could possibly work out a schedule that would allow him twelve weeks in the year to teach overseas. The elders weren't very happy about that idea, but they agreed. Three months later they came to Jack and said, "Jack, we want you to be our pastor until you no longer want to be here. But we know your heart is to train young men for ministry, and so we want to allow you to do that full time." Jack said, "How am I going to do that? I'm sixty-two years old; I don't have time to raise my support."

"We've thought of that," they said. "We plan to pay your present salary for five years, so you can go immediately to any-where in the world and start teaching. All we ask is that you begin to raise your support so we can get a senior pastor in a few years."

Jack was flabbergasted! He rushed home to tell me. Now, I have to tell you that there were many times in the past when Jack wanted to leave the pastorate. He would get so discouraged he would want to quit. And I would tell him, "No, it's not right for you to run away." But this time I saw that Jack was not running away, but running toward a new ministry, and I was very excited. Jack used to say, "When I told Carol about the opportunity the church gave me, she said, 'Jack you go pray—I'll go pack!'"

We started a new ministry, Equipping Pastors International, which enabled us to travel around the world—mostly to developing countries—and come alongside existing organizations and denominations, gathering pastors and wives together to teach and train them. Coming to one of our conferences was often the first time pastors had ever been away with their wives—and many of the wives had never had training at all. It was an exciting ministry, and our last eight years of marriage were the best.

Jack was very biblical, and he was not judgmental. Because he had been through depression, church splits, difficult ministries, and hard times himself, and had seen so much in the lives of others around the world, nothing surprised him. He often said, "There's nothing that can't be redeemed, nothing that can't be restored." Our marriage was a testimony to that belief.

Part III

My Thoughts
on Marriage

CHAPTER 12

The Seven Needs of Man

☙❦❧

IN ORDER to understand what God has to say about marriage, we need to go back to the very beginning, to the first bride and groom, to see exactly what God had in mind. These are very familiar passages, but for some reason I resisted the concepts taught here. We're told in Genesis 2 that perfect Adam, perfect man, was incomplete.

This concept was one of the most important things I had to learn in my marriage—and the most important thing I want every woman to know—because it means that the needs that Adam had, that all men have, are not sin. God created these needs in the man before the fall, before Adam and Eve first sinned.

I thought the reason my husband was in need was because he was so sinful. And I greatly resented being the one to meet his sinful needs. I wanted him to "grow up" and become completely self-sufficient. I got angry because I felt I was the one who had to "do all the work" when it came to meeting the needs in our marriage.

God had to show me that marriage is a ministry that he instituted, and by nature ministries are difficult, full of challenges, and directed at very needy people. In the ministry of marriage, he created the woman to be perfectly suited to fulfill what was lacking in the man.

We are told that in the beginning, God created man and put him into a perfect setting—the Garden of Eden.

God was pleased with all of his creation, stating that it was good. Yet concerning the man He had made He said, "It is not good for the man to be alone" (Genesis 2:18a). This was the first and only time God said that there was something lacking in His creation.

Why? Because God, in His sovereignty and according to His good pleasure, created the man with needs. Even though Adam was made in the image of God, had a perfect body, was in an ideal environment in the company of the entire animal kingdom, with a perfect intellect, a job well suited for him, and an intimate relationship with God, it wasn't enough. He had needs. Some significant areas in his life were lacking.

I have identified seven needs of the man from this chapter in Genesis. There may be more, but these are the ones I have learned in my studies. They are as follows:

1. The need for *relationship*
2. The need for *authority and respect*
3. The need to *provide*
4. The need to *protect*
5. The need for *sexual fulfillment*
6. The need for *companionship*
7. The need for *domestic help*

Man needed woman!

However, Adam didn't know he was in need. He didn't go to God and say, "Father in heaven, I need someone to help me out here. Please make someone for me." Adam was unaware of his need for a mate—just as many men are today.

God was full of compassion and mercy on this incomplete man and said, "I will make a helper suitable for him" (Genesis 2:18b). Note what this verse states:

- *God took the initiative.* He always takes the initiative when it comes to meeting our needs. He knows what we need before we do. Adam didn't say to God, "I need a wife."

- *God created.* He intentionally planned that this creation would be a "helper" for the man.

- *This creation would be "suitable."* God carefully designed her to meet the needs of the man perfectly, in an appropriate, fitting, proper, and right way.

The Naming of the Animals

Then God did a very interesting thing. He had just declared that it wasn't good for the man to be alone. But instead of immediately creating a helper for the man, He gave the man a job to do. He told the man to name the animals.

God brought all the animals that He had created to Adam, for him to give them all names—every animal, bird and beast. Fortunately he wasn't asked to name all the insects and fish. Still there were thousands and thousands of them. This required Adam to get to know each individual animal—to study its behavior, learn about its distinctive characteristics, and find out everything he could about how it lived—so he could give each one an appropriate name.

A giraffe might be called "the Long-necked One." A zebra might have been "the Striped One." Because of the variety and intricacies of God's animal kingdom, this probably took a very long time.

Why do you suppose God had Adam do this before he created the woman? I think for several reasons.

As Adam learned about each animal, he began to realize that not one of these thousands of animals was a suitable mate for him. He became more aware of his loneliness and need for someone to be his personal companion and partner.

God also wanted Adam to be fully aware that the helper He was going to give him was not to be dominated like an animal, live like an animal, or be treated like an animal.

Animals have come to be considered property, to be bought, sold, and traded. Often they are beaten, abused, and neglected. They are put in cages, fenced in, and put on tethers and leashes. They carry burdens and pull heavy loads. They are not given freedom of choice or independence and are not allowed to go where and when they please.

In many parts of the world, women are considered property, treated like animals, and are even less valuable than cattle. They are beaten and mistreated. They work in the fields, carry burdens, meet every whim of their husbands with a minimum of care in return, and are not considered smart enough to give opinions or provide advice. While not actually caged, they are not allowed the freedom they should have as one created in the image of God.

"Our Wives Like to Be Beaten"

During one marriage conference in Africa, my husband was telling the pastors why their wives should not be treated like animals. After the conference was over, one pastor stood up and said, "We didn't know it was wrong to beat our wives. We don't beat ours as much as non-Christians do, but we know now that even rare beatings are wrong." Another pastor stood up and said, "But our wives like to be beaten. It makes them think we love them." Then I stood up and said, "Have you asked your wife if she likes to be beaten?" They said they hadn't, and when they admitted they shouldn't do it again, the wives all loudly applauded!

When we travel throughout developing countries, we see that it is usually the women who are in the fields working. Many times we pass villages where men are sitting on porches in the shade, playing mancala or bao (popular games), while the women are out in the hot fields weeding and planting. When confronted about this custom, the men admit it is wrong, but the culture has dictated that garden work is woman's work.

In Uganda, women carry the luggage for us, even when we protest. At our conferences, they would carry the benches in and out of the church. Jack would teach from Peter's second epistle that the woman is the "weaker vessel." Then he would ask the men, "Who is stronger, you or your wife?" When they would admit that the men were stronger, he would ask them, "Well then, why do you have the women do the heavy lifting instead of you?" They couldn't answer, but the next time benches needed to be carried, it was the men who did it, while the women watched, beaming.

God wanted Adam to be fully aware that Eve was not an animal and wasn't to be treated like one. Meeting and inspecting each animal before naming it was an excellent way for Adam to become acquainted with them. God wanted the man to understand that when He brought a mate to him, she was not an animal and was not to be treated like an animal.

God also showed Adam that he was given the privilege to name each animal. Only those in authority have the right to give names, so God was giving Adam authority. Parents have authority over their children, therefore they have the right to name their children. Owners of businesses have the authority to name their own company. Naming implies authority, and Adam was given this authority by God.

So Adam learned many lessons during this period of naming the animals.

The Creation of Woman

After what could have been months or even years, God put Adam to sleep and, without his knowledge, prepared a wife for him. He didn't want any interference, suggestions, or proposals by Adam on the type of woman He would make. This was entirely God's doing, completely and totally planned and designed by Him.

Adam was unaware of the preparation and creation of a helper for him. He was oblivious to his own needs, and he didn't know that God was at work fashioning a perfect mate for him.

God then took out of the man a rib. The correlation between a rib and a woman is significant.

A rib is one of the most delicate and fragile bones in the human body. It is easily broken, but it protects the most important organ—the heart. In fact, a rib will bruise and crush before the heart is damaged. A woman is fragile, physically "weaker" (1 Peter 3:7), but she protects the "heart of the home."

The rib cage supports the whole body. Without ribs the body would collapse and fall. The woman supports the man, and without her strength the family would fall apart.

God did not take a bone from Adam's head, as the woman is not to dominate or rule over the man. Nor did He take a bone from the foot, as she is not to be trampled on or considered beneath the man. But God took a bone from Adam's side, as she is to stand beside him always and to be his equal; from under his arm, for she is to be protected; and close to his heart, for she is to be loved.

The animals were made out of dirt. Adam was made out of dirt. But the woman was not made out of dirt, but out of the bone of man.

God knew exactly what the man needed and took great care to make the woman perfectly suited and matched to meet the man's needs. Let's look at each of the seven needs in detail.

1 The Need for Relationship

BEFORE EVE was created, Adam did not have another creature to relate to as a person. The Father, Son, and Holy Spirit are persons, and they relate to one another. They created man as a person, made in the image of God. Animals are not persons. In order for Adam to experience a relationship to other persons on the earth and to experience love at the highest level, he needed another creature made in the image of God. He needed Eve.

This concept is captured concisely in perhaps the most clear and reliable work to date on male–female roles, the book *Recovering Biblical Manhood and Womanhood* (Wayne Grudem & John Piper, editors, Crossway Books, 1991): "Men and women are of equal value and dignity in the eyes of God—both created in the image of God and utterly unique in the universe" (p. 49).

Unlike the animals, Eve was able to relate to Adam, and vice versa, due to their mutual sense of conscience, morality, righteousness, and holiness. They related to each other as highly intelligent, rational beings as well. Also, they shared an intuitive, creative, artistic view of reality since they were both made in the image of the first Creator.

While the sexes have their differences and their particular roles of authority and submission (which I discuss in the next section), this does not in any way discount their equality as persons and bearers of the image of God as they relate to one another. *Recovering Biblical Manhood and Womanhood* says it this way: "God exists as one Godhead in three Persons, equal in glory but unequal in role. Within the Holy Trinity the Father leads, the Son submits to Him, and the Spirit submits to both (the Economic Trinity). But it is also true that the three Persons are fully equal in divinity, power, and glory (the Ontological Trinity). The Son submits, but not because He is God, Jr., an inferior deity. The ranking within the Godhead is a part of the sublime beauty and logic of true deity" (p. 103).

2 The Need for Authority and Respect

MAN AND WOMAN also relate to each other as equals but in differing roles. As *Recovering Biblical Manhood and Womanhood* notes: "There is a paradox in the creation account...God created male and female in His image equally, but He also made the male the head and the female the helper" (p. 99).

Adam was created with the need to rule. He was given authority over all the earth to "subdue" and rule over it (Genesis 1:28). Although it implies that the woman was also given this mandate, the man was the only one given the authority to name. Adam named the animals before Eve was created, and he named his helper twice. When God brought her to him, Adam called her "Woman." After she bore him a child, he named her "Eve," or "life-giver," because she was the mother of every living person to follow.

Throughout the Bible, God named and renamed people to suit His plans and distinguish his leaders. Names often designate personality, position, and characteristics and are the result of a person's actions or reactions to God's purposes. The giving of names is an incredibly important task and implies the privilege of authority.* This authority and the subsequent respect it requires has been placed in every man.

A wife's submission to her husband helps fulfill his need to exercise authority.

I remember the first time I read the verse that a wife was to be in submission to her husband. I couldn't believe it! And I certainly did not like it. I understood the concept in Ephesians 5:21, "Submit to one another out of reverence for Christ." But I was disturbed by the very next two verses, "Wives, submit to your husbands as to the Lord. For the husband is the head of the wife as Christ is the head of the church."

---

*The concept that man was given special authority prior to the fall is reaffirmed in the New Testament (1 Timothy 2:12-13).

The idea that my husband was to rule over me was offensive and unacceptable. It conjured up all kinds of thoughts of barbarians and cavemen. It certainly didn't seem appropriate for the twentieth century. So I reinterpreted those verses. I would submit when Jack was right, I rationalized, not when he was wrong or when I disagreed with him. But as I grew in knowledge and understanding, I saw that God's concept of headship was far different than mine. Submission implies disagreement, as you would not need to submit to someone you always agreed with.

It goes on to say, "Christ is the head of the church, his body, of which he is the Savior. Husbands, love your wives, just as Christ loved the church and gave himself up for her." (Ephesians 5:25). This is the concept of submission that God has ordained.

Again, *Recovering Biblical Manhood and Womanhood* provides clarification: "Women are smarter in some ways and men are smarter in some ways; women are more easily frightened in some circumstances and men are more easily frightened in others.... Boasting in either sex as superior to the other is folly. Men and women, as God created us, are different in hundreds of ways. Being created equally in the image of God means at least this: that when the so-called weakness and strength columns for manhood and for womanhood are added up, the value at the bottom is going to be the same for each" (p. 73).

The first marriage God created was a union of two lovers who wanted what was best for the other. The man ruled, the woman submitted. It was a ruling love on the man's part. It was a loving submission on the part of the wife. Because of our fallen, sinful, and distorted world, we cannot see how this relationship brings harmony and perfect unity. But when a wife submits to her husband, she is following God's order and is meeting her husband's need for authority.

Our 16-Year-Old Rebel

I struggled with the whole idea of submission to my husband, as do most of the wives I teach, wherever I go around the world. Looking back, I can recall experiences I went through that helped me see that God blessed my attempt, however feeble, to obey and submit to Jack.

When our oldest son, Mark, was 16, he was going through a rebellious stage of life. To others he was a good kid, but he wasn't interested in spiritual things and didn't want to go to church or attend the youth group activities there. He said to us, "You are trying your hardest to make me a Christian, and I'm trying my hardest not to be one!" He was well taught, however, and said to Jack, "Dad, if I'm among the elect I'll be saved. If I'm not, you can't do anything about it. So get off my back!"

It came to the point that Jack had to ask the elders in the church to pray for Mark and his attitude, because Jack knew that if Mark's rebellion continued and got worse, he would have to leave the ministry. Jack took seriously the admonition that a church leader was to have his family under control.

The elders were surprised, because Mark seemed to them to be an obedient son. But in our home, we knew how difficult Mark was making our family life, and his sullen attitude affected his brothers as well.

I knew that Mark had been going out with his friends from school and drinking a little. I didn't tell Jack. I was protecting Mark from what I knew his father would do. I thought it was a phase that all boys went through ("boys will be boys") and didn't want Jack to get any more upset with Mark than he already was.

One night Mark went out with some of his buddies and apparently had a little too much to drink. Some of the guys from church saw him, and the next morning told Jack what they had seen.

I remember I was at the Olympic Swimming Pool, where we had a membership along with several other church families. It was a hot fall day, and two friends and I were sitting at the edge of the pool, dangling our feet in the water and watching some of the younger children who were splashing around the shallow end. We were talking about everyday things mothers talk about when I looked up and saw Jack, wearing a suit and tie, marching over to where I sat.

He was livid. "Carol!" he called out. "Come here! I need to talk to you!"

I was a little embarrassed that Jack would come into the pool dressed for church, and also that he would call me over in such a brusque way. Excusing myself, I went over to the side of the pool, where there were some tables and chairs under an awning, and asked Jack, "What on earth are you doing here?"

"Carol," he said, "I just found out that Mark has been drinking, and last night he got drunk!"

"Oh," I replied, "I know he has been drinking a little now and then with some of his school friends, but I don't think it's anything to worry about."

"He got drunk!" Jack started to raise his voice. I could see that I needed to calm him down or everyone at the whole community pool would start to wonder what was going on.

"Who told you he got drunk?" I asked.

When he told me, I said, "You shouldn't take their word for it. Maybe they made a mistake. And it's not the end of the world, you know. Boys will be boys."

Well, that was the wrong thing to say, because Jack had a hatred for alcohol, stemming from seeing his own mother drunk once, when he was a little boy.

He said, "We'll see. I don't know what I'm going to do yet, but I'm not going to overlook this."

He strode out, and as I watched him go, I wondered what would happen to the tenuous relationship Mark already had with his father.

When Mark got home from school that afternoon, Jack called him on the telephone. "Mark, come up to my office. I want to talk to you."

Mark slowly walked up to the church, which was on a hill behind our house, dreading what it was that made his dad call with that harsh tone of voice. When he got to the office, he slowly went in. "Sit down, son, I need to talk to you."

"Did you go out last night and get drunk?" Jack demanded.

"No, Dad," Mark said. He thought he knew better than to confess to something he had done when confronted by an angry father.

"You weren't drinking last night with your school friends?" Jack mentioned several of them by name.

"No, Dad. You know I wouldn't do that."

"What if I told you that one of them came to me this morning and told me he saw you, talked to you?"

Mark realized he was nailed and tried unsuccessfully to back out of his denials.

One thing Jack hated more than alcohol was lying. He said to Mark, "When I heard you were out drinking and got drunk, I was going to discipline you. But now, because you lied to me, you are in serious trouble, young man."

He told Mark to go home and that he would get back to him later to tell him what he was going to do.

Around five o'clock Jack came home and said he wanted to talk to me. We went up to our bedroom.

"Carol, I am going to discipline Mark, and I want your approval," he said. "I've decided to take away the privilege of driving our car for three months, and I'm going to have him sit out basketball for the rest of the season."

Now, at that time in Mark's life, these were the only two things that he really enjoyed. He loved driving our car and would readily chauffeur whenever I needed one of his brothers taken anywhere. And basketball was his passion. He was one of the star players on the team, and they were getting ready for the playoffs, where they would have a good chance at the championship.

"You're crazy!" I said to Jack. "You can't do that! Do you want to alienate Mark and make him hate us even more?"

"I've been praying about what I should do," Jack replied. "I believe God has given me this discipline."

"No, you don't understand," I cried. "I'm his mother! I know what's best, and I know how this would affect him. We would drive him even further away. He might leave home. We might lose him completely."

Jack was adamant. "I believe this discipline is from God," he said.

I argued. I cried. I pleaded. I got angry. Jack didn't budge. I stormed out, slamming the door, and went downstairs to prepare dinner.

I have a vivid memory of this moment. I was standing over the stove, stirring boiling rice, the steam rising up to my face, and my tears flowing into the rice. I cried out to God, "Please, God! Don't let him do this!"

I heard a voice, not audible, but a clear impression on my mind, "*Carol, does it say anywhere in the Bible not to discipline by taking away the car or basketball?*"

"Of course not!" I thought.

"*Carol, does it say anywhere in the Bible, 'Wives, be in submission to your husbands'?*"

"Yes, it does say that. But it's impossible when you know, with every fiber of your being, that your husband is wrong!"

Then God spoke to me words I'll never forget, "*Carol, can't you trust Me with My Word?*"

"Oh God, I want to! But it's so hard! I'm afraid I'll lose my son!"

I went upstairs and told Jack that I would go along with his discipline, but I added, "I still think you are wrong!"

When Jack told Mark of the discipline, Mark replied, "Dad, you know you want to watch me play basketball more than I want to play it, and you know that Mom will have to drive Brian, David, and Dean to all their practices, games, and activities." This was all true.

Mark got very angry, but he didn't run away, and we didn't lose him.

In fact, it was just a few months later when Mark came to us one evening and said, "Mom and Dad, I have something to tell you. Today I gave my life to Jesus Christ."

I learned one of the most important lessons of marriage. I never needed to fear obeying God. He always blesses obedience! "Delight yourself in the Lord and He will give you the desires of your heart" (Psalm 37:4).

Submission Inside and Out

However, even though I saw God bless my submission, I was still woefully lacking in treating Jack with admiration and respect. God wanted me to understand how much Jack required these things from me, not because he was worthy, but because it was a great need that had to be met.

It was while Jack and I were at Marble Retreat that the difference between authority and respect was brought to my attention. I also learned that pride and ego are two different things, and that husbands have a great need to have their egos built. Ego is what makes a man feel like a man. It's God's business to break one's pride, not mine.

This concept was a new revelation to me, because I had deliberately kept myself from building Jack up, showing him admiration and respect, and treating him as the authority in the home.

I believed that my husband had too big of an ego, and that I shouldn't do anything to "build up his pride." I used to subtly make fun of Jack, both publicly and privately.

Jack had always been the brunt of much kidding. Many practical jokes were played on him, by both family and friends, which he usually enjoyed. Some backfired, however, like the time some teens taped down the nozzle on the kitchen sink hose, thinking I would get spray on my face the next time I turned on the tap. But Jack unexpectedly came home to take his vitamins on his way to conduct a funeral, and he was the one who got the spray—all over his suit.

Normally he could take all the pranks and jokes, but from his wife it hurt. He often told me that my remarks made him feel bad, yet I just thought he was being too sensitive.

Even though I had grasped the concept of Jack's authority over me, I was not considering his need for me to show him appreciation and respect. I discovered that even during the times I was successfully submitting to him, I was doing it grudgingly and resented it.

There were obviously many things about Jack I admired, because I had chosen him to be my husband—a voluntary act that I wanted to do. But I had lost sight of them. I was only thinking of the negatives.

Our marriage counselor reminded me to read Philippians 4:8 again, and to think about my husband: "Whatever is true, whatever is noble, whatever is right, whatever is pure, whatever is lovely, whatever is admirable—if anything is excellent or praiseworthy—think about such things."

I had been dwelling on whatever was bad, whatever was bugging me, whatever made me angry, whatever weakness he had, whatever dumb things he did, whatever unkind words he spoke. It was no wonder the love was gone! It was like I was pouring cold water on a hot fire—until the flame went out and the fire died. That was what I was doing in my heart.

As I began looking for "whatever was admirable," those qualities that made me fall in love with him, I found there were many things. I was then asked by the counselor to tell Jack about them, and when I did, I saw his attitude change and his self-esteem increase.

Before we were married, I complimented Jack often, admired him, and gave him a lot of positive strokes. I wanted him to feel good around me, so that he would spend more time with me, and then eventually ask me to marry him. It worked.

But not long after marriage I stopped admiring him. I didn't tell him nice things about what he did or how he looked. I stopped appreciating anything he did for me. He wasn't receiving the admiration or respect that I had previously given, and it hurt him. Husbands need respect, and if they don't get it from their wives, they will listen to other women who will give it to them. Most affairs begin when a man receives admiration and respect from another woman. That's why God clearly tells us that "the wife must see to it that she respects her husband" (Ephesians 5:33, NASB).

There is a correlation between submission and respect, but they are not the same thing. I know many women who outwardly look meek and submissive, but in their heart they are seething with bitterness and hostility. I was like that for many years.

God says that a woman is to have a "gentle and quiet spirit" (1 Peter 3:4). However, don't confuse that with personality. I often worried that I was too boisterous and lively in conversation, but God was not displeased with my tendency to be fun-loving. He was concerned with the attitude of my heart.

When the Holy Spirit convicted me of my lack of appreciation of Jack, and I began to show him the admiration he needed, deliberately making a choice to respect him, it was a turning point in my marriage. It didn't have anything to do with whether Jack was worthy or not, it was all about my obedience and whether I was fulfilling my calling and ministry to be my husband's helper.

3 *The Need to Provide*

GOD PUT ADAM into the garden of Eden to work it (Genesis 2:15). Gardens, even in a perfect world, need to be cultivated. Adam was to keep busy—planting, trimming, pruning, and picking. This job would occupy much of his time and energy. It gave him great pleasure to see how this beautiful garden developed and produced food.

Man was created by God to work, to be the provider. It is part of his Creator's design. A man without a job does not feel like a complete man. This is a problem in a world filled with unemployment and joblessness.

Women do not have this same need. That is why God states that the primary activity for married women and mothers is to be homemakers (Titus 2:5). When women fill the jobs that men need, it causes all sorts of problems. That doesn't mean that it's wrong for a woman to work outside the home, as along as she is able to care for her family first.

The Proverbs 31 woman had all kinds of jobs and activities. She sewed garments to clothe her family and to sell at market, she made profits in real estate, she planted vineyards, she did volunteer work in the community, she traveled, and she was able to dress in the latest styles. But in all this, her first and primary ministry was to her husband (Proverbs 31:11-12).

But what often happens is that women, who many times are more qualified and capable than men, take jobs in the workforce, and it leaves fewer jobs for men. And men *need* to work. It is part of their makeup. It makes them feel significant. If they don't work, they are incomplete. They feel they have no value. That isn't a problem with women, who are able to fill up their time with many activities, both inside and outside the home.

Throughout the world, women are getting educated, liber-ated, and empowered, which is a good thing. In Africa, however, what I see happening is the unemployment rate among men rising to alarming levels, which is causing tension in the home, a rise in crime, abuse, and neglect. Idle men often become gamblers and drunkards. Men out of work move to the big cities to try to find jobs, away from their families, and then often contract AIDS, which they take home to their wives. They resort to criminal activity. Without money they look for opportunities to steal and rob. And because they are unfulfilled, they become angry and rebellious, prime targets for riots, insurgencies, and civil wars.

Often women take jobs just to get out of the house and get away from the mundane chores that are found there. Taking care of a family and managing a home can become boring, routine, and tiring, and it can seem unfulfilling. While the mother's excuse is to earn money needed to raise a family, most children would trade material things for the daily presence of their mother.

While in seminary, Jack didn't work. Because he wasn't raised in a Christian home, he thought he needed to catch up on all the truths he had missed out on growing up. He used every spare minute he had to study diligently, often late into the night.

Before we were married, Jack and I had the conviction that I would stay home when children came. I had planned to work while Jack was in seminary. But when I unexpectedly got pregnant after two months of marriage, our resolve was put to the test. We didn't know how we were going to make it, but we made the decision that I would stay home and take care of the baby. We were aware of the saying, "The devil doesn't care if you have convictions as long as you don't put them into practice." We didn't know how God was going to provide, but we believed our conviction was from Him, so we trusted that our needs would be met.

We were receiving enough from the McManis Fund to pay the rent, utilities, food, and gasoline. But there was very little left over for anything else. But for five years, before Jack took his first church, we saw God provide in miraculous ways.

We never needed medical care. Our car never needed to go to a mechanic. Few things got broken in the home. Our clothes stayed in style or were replaced by the free "clothes closet" for seminary students our church provided. Church members regularly took us out to dinner and a movie, understanding the financial situation we were in.

We deprive ourselves of seeing God perform miracles when we take matters into our own hands and try to provide for ourselves in ways that jeopardize our family. Those years with our boys can never be given back. And they don't last that long. It wasn't easy, I admit that, but it was the right thing to do, and God blessed us for it.

The children in Africa don't have many material things. There isn't even a word for "toy" in Swahili. There the boys make soccer balls out of banana leaves or tightly wrapped plastic bags. They invent games with sticks and seeds. The girls play jacks using small pebbles, throwing a stone up and catching it without a bounce. They don't need to play with dolls, because even the very young girls take care of real babies.

Rarely do you see children cry in Africa. They don't whine or complain. They are usually happy and content, even in the midst of dismal poverty. They have shown me that lavishing material goods on our children doesn't necessarily mean it will make them happier. Plus, we need to ask ourselves, do we want to make our children happy—or holy?

For men, work is not a bad thing, a punishment, but a fulfilling of the mandate given to them by their Creator. It makes them feel more like a man to be the main provider for their family. Work is from the hand of God and is a gift of God (Ecclesiastes 2:24; 5:19).

Jack stayed at Grace Church for over sixteen years, often struggling with the ministry, sometimes painfully, because he didn't want to jeopardize the security of the family. He might have gone off on some other tangent that could have brought him more fulfillment, but he would not have had the security of the income.

When we did go to Kernersville and all of a sudden there was no job, no money, and no security, he was at his lowest point in our marriage. In large part he was depressed because he wasn't able to provide for the family.

Then I went to work. It was the first time since our first year of marriage that I held a steady nine-to-five job, bringing in the only income. It wasn't normal. He hated it, that I was the one who was making the money while he was staying home.

During one trip to Africa, Jack and I took a seven-hour bus trip from Mombasa to Lamu in Kenya. My sister has a home, workshop, gallery, and guesthouse there. We left early in the morning; the bus was packed with luggage, crates, and boxes, as well as men, women, and children. My sister had arranged for us to sit up front because Jack had such long legs. Between us and the driver was a hard plastic cover for the gearbox or something. A young boy, about seven years old, was placed on that hard box by his mother, who had the seat behind us.

For the duration of the whole trip, that boy sat there, except for one stop halfway. He never whined or complained. He never said, "When will we get there?" or "I'm tired!" or "I'm bored."

I'm telling you this because I think that children in America are indulged and given material possessions far beyond what they need or require. It takes money to live, but it's usually the extra, nonessential, material things that make a woman think she needs to go to work to make money for her children.

Staying home when the children are young, doing without the unnecessary items, would produce more jobs for men and enable them to fulfill their need to be the provider in the family.

4 The Need to Protect

GOD NOT ONLY had Adam work in the Garden, He also put him in the Garden to guard and protect it. The man was given the responsibility to guard and protect that which belongs* to him: his wife, his family, his home, his land, his country. Man will fight to protect these if he is in danger of losing them or if they are threatened by outside forces. That is why there are wars, because men will fight to keep that which belongs to them. It is part of their Creator's design, contorted and complicated by the fall.

Throughout the world, men are the aggressive ones when it comes to guarding and protecting. In Kenya, there are men who stand guard at the entrance of every business, company, store, apartment complex, and hotel. (They say that one-third of Kenya guards one-third of the country from the other third.)

Most women don't want to fight. We will protect our immediate family and home, but when it comes to waging war, most women would rather just live in peace and give up their possessions.

When our children were small, Jack felt it was important to get term life insurance. I thought it was a waste of money, as I was raised in a family that didn't believe in insurance. We had many heated discussions about the cost of having this protection.

I used to argue with Jack even more about a full-blown insurance policy. I thought it was a great expense, considering our meager income. I didn't want him worth more dead than alive. I always thought that if anything ever happened to him, I could manage on my own. I didn't see the need to spend that kind of money to protect the family in case he died. I felt the same about medical insurance. We were a pretty careful family,

---

* In using the word "belongs," I am not speaking of ownership in the ultimate sense, but rather responsible stewardship over that which God has entrusted to us. He is the "owner," and we are the stewards of those things that "belong" under our care and responsibility.

and we had been spared most medical expenses. I just felt like it was a tremendous waste of money, and I would tell him so. It would hurt him, because he felt compelled to spend the money, even though I disapproved.

I'm not interested in financial affairs. Although I did all the bookkeeping in our home, I've never been interested in investments, portfolios, insurance, and things like that.

Then I became aware of the need God gave man to be the protector, and I realized that buying life insurance was one of the ways Jack was trying to be the protector of his family. Instead of arguing with him, I understood why he was doing it and thanked him for his care and concern for me and the boys. So I had to acquiesce and let him know I supported his desire to be a responsible protector. My change of attitude encouraged him to be an even better provider.

A few years ago we were going over our finances. Jack wanted to increase his life insurance policy. I protested. He explained again to me how important it was for him to know I would be taken care of if and when he died. I have to admit now how helpful that insurance fund was when I had the expenses of his memorial service and burial.

Jack, the Knife

One evening, while we were in seminary, I was driving home alone, late at night, from a wives' fellowship meeting. I stopped at a red light and glanced at the driver of the car next to me. The man looked at me, and our eyes met. I quickly looked away, and when the light turned green, I was troubled to see him following me.

When I turned onto Ferguson Road, he turned also. It was a dark and lonely street, and just before I got to the house, he pulled alongside of me and tried to push me off the road. I was able to turn into our driveway, and I ran into the house, shaken.

I told Jack what had happened, and he was very disturbed that someone had attempted to push me off the road, probably with bad intentions. We agreed that when I was driving at night alone, I should never look into the faces of other drivers.

Within hours, there was a pounding on the door in the middle of the night. I was frightened—I thought this was the man returning. "Who's there?" Jack asked, and the only answer was, "Open the door!"

Jack went into the kitchen and got a butcher knife, which really made me scared! He told the man to go away, and that he had a knife and would use it if he tried to break in. Moments later we learned that it was a taxi driver who had driven a man to our house, and that he had disappeared in the neighborhood behind our house. The driver was only trying to get his money.

This made me realize the lengths my husband would go to protect me. At the time it worried me, but later I learned that he was exercising his God-given design.

I had a hard time accepting Jack's need to be my protector. I am a very independent, strong-willed, and proud world traveler. I can take care of myself and don't like to ask for help.

Several times Jack would comment that he felt I didn't need him. It hurt him, and I would say it wasn't true, but in my heart I did feel that way.

One of our first trips to Africa was right after my ninety-one-year-old father had hip-replacement surgery. I was concerned about how he was doing and if he had gone home from the hospital. We were far out in the country of Uganda where there was no power (or running water, for that matter), no telephones, and obviously no e-mail.

I had been told that our final week (our seventh) would be in a town that had a "one-star hotel" with power and telephones, so I would finally be able to call California and find out about my father. I was looking forward to talking to my sister after six weeks of no communication.

We left the village where we had been conducting a marriage conference for several hundred Pentecostal pastors and wives. It was a two-hour drive to the town where we would have our next conference. As we drove from the dirt road onto the main paved road, I noticed leaning power poles along the way, with one thin wire strung along the top. I thought, "This skinny wire is bringing power to the town, but it doesn't look very adequate!"

We arrived at the hotel in the late afternoon. I couldn't wait for my first hot shower in two and a half weeks. Then I would make a telephone call, factoring in the ten-hour time difference. We were warmly received at the reception desk, and as they escorted us to our room they said, "We are so sorry, but the whole town has been without power for three days, and therefore we have no pumps to run the water system, no lights, and no telephone service."

We went into our darkened room, which had been supplied with candles, a kerosene lantern, and two buckets of water, one warm to bathe with and one cold to flush the toilet with. I sat down on one of the beds, with the mattress so thin I could feel the slats under it, and broke into tears. Jack sat down next to me and put his arm around me. I laid my head on his shoulder and said, "I want to go home."

Jack later told me it was one of the few times he ever remembers having to comfort me in a difficult situation—and it made him feel good!

5 The Need for Sexual Fulfillment

ONE OF THE greatest and strongest needs God has put into man is the sex drive. This is God's doing. He thought up the sex act, procreation, the pleasure of intimacy, and the union of "one flesh" (Genesis 2:24).

Life before men as a mere high school girl (left) and later as a slightly wiser sorority gal (below).

When I first met Jack I thought he was so handsome.

I attended many Bible studies like this one with Vonette Bright, when Campus Crusade was just beginning.

Jack (bottom right) played for UCLA just before they won ten National Championships under legendary coach John Wooden (top left).

Engaged.

Our wedding day—young, happy,
and in love.

It didn't take long for the relationship
to become strained.

A new pastor's wife puts on a
happy face.

I loved being a mom.

I loved him and sometimes I didn't.
Was he Dr. Jack or Mr. Hyde?

Time alone was becoming rare.

A pastor in Roanoke, Virginia, a busy wife, teenage sons—
a great way to complicate a challenged marriage.

Jack's depression became clear at Rehoboth Beach. I still kept my distance.

Hurting marriage, happy faces. In Greenville our situation was critical.

At Marble Retreat in Colorado, I had my first breakthrough in conquering resentment.

But when I enjoyed life the most, it was without Jack.

In Orlando (Sea World) we started
having fun together.

Eventually our smiles
became genuine.

I said Mickey Mouse saved our marriage . . .
. . . but Jack thought it was a goofy idea.

We were a great team in ministry. Jack was a cheerleader who encouraged me to give my talk to women everywhere about overcoming resentment.

After 47 years of marriage, we took our first trip together that was not ministry or family related. This "second honeymoon" in Portland was our last photo together before Jack died six weeks later.

Adam was commanded to "be fruitful and multiply." Only a wife can properly satisfy man's innate drive to propagate the human race and to consummate intimacy between the male and female without causing the husband to sin.

Many other women can meet this need, but a wife is the only woman in the world who can be intimate with her husband without wounding his conscience and making him guilty before a holy God.

I don't know why God put such a strong sex drive in men. That's a question I will ask Him when I get to heaven. But I know that God is the one who placed it there. He thought up the sex act and delights to see a man and wife enjoy the intimacy and oneness that sexual activity brings to a healthy marriage.

Like most newlyweds, Jack and I really enjoyed sex when we were first married, but it wasn't too long after Jack and I were wed that I became less and less interested in meeting his sexual needs. I was newly pregnant, often nauseated with morning sickness (which lasted all day), and tired after working from nine to five. Going to bed with my husband was the last thing on my mind.

I was quite the expert at making excuses, and poor Jack just went back to his desk and continued studying.

God says the marriage bed is "undefiled" (Hebrews 13:4). There is nothing sinful or unholy about a man and wife giving sexual fulfillment to each other. Adam and Eve were intimately enjoying each other in the Garden of Eden long before sin entered the world.

The enemies of God are on a mission to destroy God's good gifts to His people. The pleasure of sexual activity is one of God's great gifts to mankind, but God knows best and has revealed plainly the context in which that activity is to be enjoyed. God gave us His law—"You shall not commit adultery (any sexuality outside marriage)"—because he knows the danger and destruction that comes when immorality becomes part of a society. He wants to spare us the misery of infidelity, because He loves us.

Many times I would ask God why my desire to meet Jack's needs for sexual fulfillment was woefully deficient. I usually blamed Jack's lack of sensitivity toward my needs. If he wasn't going to help me, then I wouldn't help him. But it seemed to me that I was unusually uninterested compared to what I saw on TV and what I would hear from others.

Was it because Jack wasn't a good husband? I knew he was trying to please God in his marriage, and I also knew that there were a lot of husbands out there much worse than mine.

Was it because there was something wrong with me? Was I undersexed in an oversexed world?

Was it because I had come to Christ at the age of twenty, and Jack wasn't my first sexual experience? I knew God's standard, and I had not kept it before becoming a Christian.

I remember pleading with God, "It would be so much easier to be a good wife if you gave me some interest, some desire, some passion for Jack!"

It got to the point where I never wanted to hug Jack, even though I longed for affection, because I knew it would give him ideas and lead straight to the bedroom.

When I did meet his sexual needs, I knew in my heart that I had done the right thing, that I had pleased not only my husband, but also God. And Jack was so much easier to live with.

A sexually unfulfilled husband cannot be a good husband. He gets angry, irritated easily, and frustrated. Often Jack would take his frustration out on the children instead of me, when I knew I was the one who had caused his dissatisfaction.

Our marriage became a vicious cycle. The more I froze up on Jack, the more angry and withdrawn he became, which made me even more insensitive and remote. I believe his depression wasn't just overwork or problems on the job or midlife crisis. I know that if I had been a supportive, caring, and sympathetic wife, Jack would have had the encouragement and strength to tackle the world.

It is extremely difficult for men to handle the struggles and hardships of life alone. That's one of the reasons God created women. A wise wife, one who "builds her house" rather than tearing it down, will understand the power she has to help her husband cope with whatever circumstances he faces.

Often wives use sex as a weapon, either to reject or entice. What a ploy of God's enemies!

When I came to the place in my marriage where I wanted to please God by meeting the needs of my husband, I determined that I would not reject his advances. There were times when I said, "Not now—later." But I knew that rejection is painful and cruel for a man to experience, and so I tried very hard to meet all Jack's needs for sexual fulfillment.

Even then, I often did not want to give my body to my husband, even though I'm told in 1 Corinthians 7:4, "The wife's body does not belong to her alone, but also to her husband." But then I would think of Christ, agonizing in the Garden of Gethsemane, who didn't want to give his body either, but He did, because it was the right thing to do.

That may seem like a ridiculous comparison, but for me it gave me the desire to fulfill God's will for me in return for the huge sacrifice that Christ made for me.

The words of Romans 12:1 was such a help in giving me that determination. It says that I can "offer my body as a living sacrifice, holy and pleasing to God," and that it is a "spiritual act of worship" when I do so.

And, like many acts of obedience, over time I often received my own personal reward and satisfaction, after being concerned with pleasing God and others first. Over time, as I became more faithful to meeting his sexual needs, he became more sensitive to my romantic needs, and he became a better lover.

When Jack and I would teach our marriage conferences around the world, he would state over and over again, "God's way is one man with one woman, in the bonds of marriage, for a lifetime." He would go on to explain that God's way not only ensured a happy and healthy marriage, but it also prevented AIDS. Many pastors in Africa had never known that before.

I'm so grateful that God enabled me to learn these lessons before it was too late, before that fateful day in January 2005. The regret would have grieved me too much.

6 The Need for Companionship

WHEN GOD SAID, "It is not good for the man to be alone" (Genesis 2:18), He was stating that a man needs a companion to partner with him in life. A man gets lonely. He can perform better when he knows his wife is on his side. This need is similar to the first, the need to relate, but I view companionship on a more practical, day-to-day level.

When Jack had an early-morning meeting, he would often get up, go into the kitchen, and fix himself scrambled eggs, toast, juice, and coffee. He enjoyed eating, and he didn't mind fixing his own breakfast if I wanted to sleep. But if I was out of town, he would go to Denny's! When I asked him why he didn't fix his own breakfast when I was gone, he said, "I don't like eating in an empty house."

Men don't like being lonely. Even if they are in another room, ignoring the family, absorbed in their own world, they like the fact that there is someone in the house with them. It's a fact of life.

God has made man to need companionship. "She is your partner, the wife of your marriage covenant" (Malachi 2:14).

Jack didn't like being alone. God said it first, "It is not good for man to be alone." Most men need a partner, a companion, someone to "be there" for them. The presence of a wife in the home gives a husband the confidence that "all's right with the world."

Women also need companionship, but that need can also be met by other women. When Mary found out she was pregnant with baby Jesus, she was frightened, confused, and unsure of what to do. She didn't go to Joseph exclusively for advice and comfort; she went to Elizabeth, another woman, who would be able to understand and counsel her. Women connect with other women; men often do not understand women very well.

When we were first married, Jack worked on weekends as a Little League baseball umpire. He had to drive to the ball fields, and he was terrible with directions. He always wanted me to go along with him, to keep him company and help him find the park. At first I got angry at Jack's inability to find his way around, read a map, or follow directions. Then I realized that was one of the reasons God put us together. He needed my expertise in getting us to our destination, and I learned to appreciate those strengths he had to help my weaknesses and shortcomings. But he also just wanted my company.

Companions often are opposites, and instead of making this fact a source of friction, like I did at the beginning of our marriage, we should applaud the differences and realize that this is why God puts us with someone who can complement and complete us.

When Jack and I conducted our marriage conferences around the world, we would conclude the four-day events with a little skit, telling the people how different we were. It went as follows (see next page):

Jack would say:	Then Carol would respond:
I grew up in a family of all boys.	I grew up in a family of all girls.
My family were strong Republicans.	My family were liberal Democrats.
I played basketball, football, baseball, and tennis all through school.	I played flute, took ballet, and belonged to Symphony for Youth.
I wore the same blue denims and cotton shirts every day in high school.	I changed outfits two to three times every morning and followed every fad.
I rarely listened to the radio or records or cared much about music.	I loved rhythm & blues and bought every new record that came out.
I grew up eating meat and potatoes.	I ate stir-fry, rice, tofu, and sprouts.
I like to sleep without any covers except a sheet.	I sleep in a flannel nightgown with a heavy comforter over me.
I like war movies and hate fantasy.	I love fantasies and hate war movies.
My idea of an ideal vacation is to go off by myself and fish.	My idea of a great vacation is to visit family and friends and party every day.
I like to go to bed early.	I like to go to bed late.
I don't like to read in bed.	I love to read in bed.

Jack (continued):	Carol (continued):
I'm a type A, high-strung, driven clock-watcher.	I'm a laid-back, easygoing, mañana-type person.
—	—
I don't like surprises or new adventures.	I love surprises and new adventures.
—	—
I like television.	I hate television.
—	—
I like to be early to airports, meetings, and appointments.	I like to do everything last minute.
—	—
I like my pizza thick and chewy.	I like mine thin and crispy.
—	—
I don't like to miss a meal.	I rarely get hungry.
—	—
When I teach I want my content well thought-out, researched, and written up.	I like to "wing it."
—	—
I believe marriage is forever.	I believe marriage is forever.
—	—
I believe marriage is hard and takes work.	I believer marriage is hard and takes work.
—	—
My desire is to please God in my marriage.	My desire is to please God in my marriage.
—	—
The Bible is my foundation for living.	The Bible is my foundation for living.

Then we would say in unison:

Christ is my strength, and through Him I can do all things.

This was always a hit with the people, and you could tell by their reactions that most of them were opposites of their mates as well.

Jack loved to fish. He grew up in a family that owned a small fishing boat, and often they would go together to the Colorado River or Salton Sea to spend several days camping and fishing.

He was also an athlete and loved all sports, especially basketball. He had trophies and medals from high school where he participated in basketball, football, baseball, tennis, and track (something that you could do at a small school like Barstow High School in the middle of the Mojave Desert).

I had very limited experience with any sport. I don't think I attended but a handful of football games at my high school, and then it was to watch the drill team, band, and cheer-leaders during halftime. I was passionate about ballet (en pointe at age nine), art, and music. I played the flute, was a member of the Los Angeles Symphony for Youth, and attended many concerts at the Hollywood Bowl. We had our own family box, and I loved going there for ballet performances under the stars.

When Jack and I got married, which of all these activities do you think we attended? I learned to fish, became a sports enthusiast (although I can hear my family laughing at that), and attended hundreds of basketball, football, and baseball games. I watched tennis matches when Jack played mixed doubles with another young girl, and even went with him when he umpired at Little League games during seminary, so he could earn a few dollars. If I had a nickel for every hard bleacher (or pew) I've ever sat in, I'd be a rich woman.

For his part, we went to a couple of concerts together, an art gallery or two, and one opera. But Jack never went to the ballet.

7 The Need for Domestic Help

ONE OF THE hardest aspects of the ministry of marriage I had to deal with was the whole concept of "mothering."

The man was to "leave his father and mother...and become one flesh" with his wife (Genesis 2:24).

When a baby boy is born, all his needs are met by his parents. Much time and energy is spent, mostly by the mother, making sure he has good, nutritious food, clean clothes, a place to sleep, and lots of love. He is nursed and cared for when he is sick. When he gets hurt, he is comforted. When he is sad, he is encouraged. When he goes off to school, he is given the confidence to do his best, and when he does well, he is told, "We're so proud of you!"

All these are needed to make him a happy and healthy boy.

Do these needs go away when a boy grows up and gets married? No, they don't. But he is to "leave his mother and father." So who is to meet these needs now? The wife!

I was thinking, "I have four little boys of my own to take care of! I don't want to have to mother my six-foot-three husband!"

So God had to teach me that Jack still needed some of the same type of care, concern, comfort, and "mothering" that was given to him by his parents.

Remember, this need is not a sin. If you look upon the needs of your husband as weaknesses, shortcomings, sins, and failings, then you will become bitter and resent your role as helper. Men are very needy, even if they don't recognize it—like Adam. It is much easier for them to function properly when the wife meets these needs.

My change in attitude made me realize that doing humdrum, everyday tasks is very important. Billy Graham called it the "godly mundane." I then understood that the ordinary things were pleasing to God and were part of my ministry, so I could do them with joy and perseverance and gratitude.

Recovering Biblical Manhood and Womanhood provides a superb definition of femininity: "At the heart of mature femininity is a freeing disposition to affirm, receive, and nurture strength and leadership from worthy men in ways appropriate to a woman's differing relationships" (p. 46).

The book goes on to define the word *nurture* in detail: "Nurture means that a mature woman senses a responsibility not merely to receive, but to nurture and strengthen the resources of masculinity. She is to be his partner and assistant. She joins in the act of strength and shares in the process of leadership. She is, as Genesis 2:18 says, 'a helper suitable for him'" (p. 48-49).

Sacrificing my Body

It's vitally important to know your husband well in order to meet his needs. It was many years before I learned that Jack got low blood sugar if he didn't eat, and it made him harsh and irritated. I knew I had to "walk on eggshells" around him before dinner, but it didn't dawn on me that it had something to do with his need for food. When I finally learned this, I never wanted him to go hungry.

There was an incident that seems funny now, but at the time it was embarrassing and not in the least bit funny. It was two days before Arny (our third son) and Jan's wedding in Greenville, South Carolina. Our second son, Brian, was flying into Atlanta, and no one was available to pick him up, so I told Jack he had to go. This troubled him greatly, as he wasn't good with directions, it was a two-hour drive to Atlanta, and he hadn't had lunch. He became so disturbed that he wouldn't even eat the sandwich I had prepared for him. As he began to leave, I told him I didn't want him to go without eating, because I knew how angry it would make him, and it was a long drive. He stormed out anyway and got in the car. I ran after him with the wrapped sandwich in my hand. He locked the car door and wouldn't take the sandwich, out of spite. So, to keep him from leaving in this angry state without eating, I laid down under the wheels of the car. Just then, our neighbor walked by. He looked at us, horrified, and asked if there was anything wrong. From under the car I said, "Oh no, we're fine!" It made Jack get out of the car long enough for me to put the sandwich on the seat beside him, which he ate an hour down the road, and then met Brian at the airport a happy man.

Don't Neglect Your Sleep or Your Husband

Jack liked going to bed early. I like to stay up late. I don't need a lot of sleep. Jack thought if he only had seven hours and fifty-nine minutes of sleep, he didn't have a good night's rest. He used to get upset that I stayed up late and couldn't understand that I didn't need more sleep.

Many times I would go to bed with him, but as soon as he fell asleep I would get back up—sometimes staying up until one or two in the morning. But then I would have the challenge of getting back into bed without waking him.

He could nap anywhere. I've seen him fast asleep in a moving pickup truck, bouncing and swerving on a rutted African road. Jack could sleep right through all the jostling. But if I quietly slipped into bed at one in the morning, he would wake up and say, "What time is it? Why are you just now going to bed?"

Once as I was rolling over to get comfortable he said, in his sleep, "Can you be still, if it's in your repertoire?"

I learned after twenty-seven years of marriage why he didn't want me to stay up late. It made him feel neglected.

He needed my attention, just like a boy needs the affirmation of his mother. Feeling neglect is a powerful emotion, and I discovered that a wise wife should do as much as possible to keep her husband from feeling neglected.

Husbands Can be Different

I have a wonderful friend, Esther, who was a good and faithful wife and mother. She and her husband had not been married very long and were living at that time in a tiny three-room duplex. Esther worked hard to keep their small home neat and clean, take good care of their two small children, and be a submissive wife, with very little income.

One day her husband came home and saw the house in disarray—toys strewn about the floor, a pile of laundry on the sofa needing to be folded, a few dishes in the sink, and dinner not ready. He got angry and told her he felt she neglected him over the children. When she asked him why he felt neglected, it came down to one simple task: ironed shirts in the closet. He said, "When I look in the closet and see clean ironed shirts, I feel that you love me and care for me, and I don't feel neglected!"

Every husband has different things that are important to them and make them feel neglected or cared for. A wise wife will discover what those things are, and if those things are done, a lot of other things can be neglected.

My wise mother told me that early in their marriage there were many days when she would spend the day reading, sewing, or playing with her three girls. When my father would come home at night, after a hard day's work during the Depression, he wanted to eat dinner. There were nights when my mother had not prepared supper and didn't even know what she was going to fix, but when she heard my father pull into the driveway, she would run to the kitchen, put an iron skillet on high heat, and cut up onions into the hot pan. My father would walk into the house, smell the frying onions, and feel that all was right with the world. He didn't feel neglected. Wise woman, my mother.

As I travel around the world, I see men who are like cripples—incomplete men—because their wives are not meeting their needs.

A man whose needs are not being met is an unhappy man. He is an angry man. He is harsh and mean. But a man whose needs are being met by an understanding wife is a happy husband. He's a better father. And he's a better provider in whatever work he is called to do.

A wise woman will understand this and build up her husband. "The wise woman builds her house, but with her own hands the foolish one tears hers down" (Proverbs 14:1).

I admit it takes a little practice to learn how to meet your own husband's particular domestic needs. Not all men are alike. On the second night of our honeymoon, Jack and I were going to a small, rustic café near our cabin for dinner. Before we got dressed to go out, I went to the closet where Jack had hung his clothes and pulled out a shirt, a matching sweater, and a pair of slacks. I carefully laid them on the bed.

Jack asked me, "What are you doing?"

I replied, "I'm laying out the clothes that you should wear tonight." I told him my mother always laid out my father's clothes because he often didn't know the type of event they were going to or what clothes would be appropriate.

Jack said to me, "I'm not your father! I can dress myself, thank you very much!" (But his tone of voice didn't seem all that thankful.)

Several months later, Jack had to remind me of this again, but in a different situation.

On the other hand, I assumed that all men could build, assemble, fix, or repair anything, like my civil engineer/inventor father. When it became apparent that Jack was not the least bit handy around the house, I got really upset. He sat me down and said to me, "Look, I'm not your father. I'm not a handyman like your father. You didn't marry your father! So make your peace with it!"

So I became Mrs. Fix-it after that.

CHAPTER 13

Eve Deceived

WOMEN TODAY want to improve their surroundings.

Whenever Jack and I moved to a new apartment or house, the first thing I wanted to do after moving in was to put pictures up on the wall. We never had enough money to redecorate, but with the familiar photos and paintings in place, it then seemed like home.

One apartment really needed curtains to keep the neighbors from looking in. I couldn't spend the money to buy them, so I rented a sewing machine for $10 a month to make them from material that was given to me. That was a lot of money—when you considered we paid $50 a month rent on the apartment. Every day I planned to start sewing, but the urgencies of the day kept me from sitting down and starting. At the end of the month, I sheepishly returned the machine, curtains unmade and precious money gone. The desire to improve my surroundings was there, but I couldn't carry through with it.

Women have always wanted to improve their surroundings. They want to change them for the better. This has been true from the very beginning.

The nineteenth-century preacher John Angell James stated, "The greatest influence on earth, whether for good or evil, is possessed by woman."

The French philosopher Alexis de Tocqueville wrote, "Morals are the work of women."

Proverbs 14:1 states it this way, "The wise woman builds her house, but with her own hands the foolish one tears hers down." The power to build or destroy is here in our hands, in our own abilities and intentions.

Women have a vital role in holding society together. It is essential for us to understand our role, our design, our biblical purpose, and our power to change the community in which God has placed us.

Whether we are married or single, divorced or widowed, we have a major role in our society as women of truth. And this role can only be properly understood from God's revelation to us in the Bible.

As Susan Hunt states in her book, *True Woman,* "This female strength will become a destructive weakness if our faith is based solely on feeling and excitement rather than on God's truth."

Liberation, God's Way

Today, women are often making changes based on feelings, emotions, worldly philosophies, and selfish motives, rather than on God's Word. Biblical truth goes against the world's thinking, so it is getting harder and harder to understand our God-given role and design.

I don't know about you, but I don't feel like helping my husband very often, and I'm certainly not excited about being a "helpmate." But I cannot base my faith on my feelings. It must be based on God's Word.

So we need to see what the Bible has to say about this. The third chapter of Genesis tells the story.

God put Adam and Eve together in the perfect garden setting. They were enjoying each other as "one flesh." They had everything they wanted to eat. They could play with the animals, pick flowers, enjoy the weather. They didn't even need to worry about what to wear.

They were "naked but not ashamed." Not only were their bodies without clothing, but their minds were completely open and honest before God, without any guilt or embarrassment.

God—almighty, all powerful, all loving, all merciful and faithful—created for Adam and Eve exactly what they needed to live forever in peace and contentment. Eden is the word we use to describe paradise—a perfect setting, a perfect environment.

Adam and Eve should have been perfectly satisfied and happy, as it is stated that their surroundings were not just good, but *very* good. They should have been able to live "happily ever after."

Our Enemy, the Deceiver

Genesis 3 tells the rest of the story. There was someone else in Eden.

Satan, the father of lies and great deceiver, was in the garden and had a mission to destroy God's perfect plan for Adam and Eve. He hated God, he hated God's creation, and he hated this first union God had put together.

However, Satan faced a difficult challenge, because neither Adam nor Eve had a sin nature. We are more easily swayed to sin, because we have a sin nature, but in Eden there was no sin yet inherent in mankind.

But because Satan was crafty and tricky, he decided to carry out his plan by using the strengths and weaknesses of the woman—her strength as the perfect helper to the man, and her weakness as one who was trusting of others and would therefore be more easily deceived.

Satan came to the woman and planted seeds of discontent by pointing out that she was missing something good, something God was keeping from her. He asked, "Did God really say, 'You must not eat from any tree in the garden'?" (Genesis 3:1). Questioning God's Word with half-truths is Satan's first avenue of temptation. He was throwing doubt on whether God had their best interests at heart, or whether God was keeping good things from them.

Satan uses this exact same tactic today, especially with young people, making them think God is against pleasure and enjoyment, and that His laws keep us from true happiness.

Eve replied with a half-truth of her own. "We may eat fruit from the trees in the garden, but God did say, 'You must not eat the fruit from the tree that is in the middle of the garden, and you must not touch it, or you will die.'" She replied that God had said not even to touch the fruit.

No, God had given this specific command to Adam before Eve was created, "You are free to eat from any tree in the garden, but you must not eat from the tree of the knowledge of good and evil, for when you eat of it you will surely die" (Genesis 2:16-17).

I believe God gave this command for two reasons. First, He wanted Adam to learn obedience and to recognize that even though He had given Adam authority over the animals, God was still in authority over him. Without a law to obey, Adam would not have been able to learn obedience.

Secondly, God wanted to protect Adam from the knowledge of the struggle between good and evil, the forces of light and the forces of darkness. He wanted Adam and Eve to live forever in perfect innocence and naïveté. Just as a parent will hide the eyes of a child in the presence of wickedness, so God wanted to keep the knowledge of evil away from Adam.

This tells me that God's laws are based on his love. He knows what is best, and He wants to protect us from evil and harm. His laws are righteous, just, and good, to help us and keep us from destroying our lives.

It was Adam's responsibility to tell Eve. But God didn't say not to touch the fruit. Either Adam misstated the law to Eve or she added to God's law.

This is often what man does. We are so afraid that people (especially our children) will break God's laws that we add to them conditions that He never intended. God gives a law and then man adds to it, making it stricter than the original rule.

When our boys were young teens, our church had the belief that it was wrong for Christians to dance. One spring their school was planning a dance in the gymnasium, and they asked if they could go. We said, "Sure, go to the dance, have a good time, and come home right afterward."

Some church members found out that we were letting our boys go to a dance, and they confronted Jack about it. "Where in the Bible does it say that kids can't dance?" he asked them.

"Well, nowhere," they replied. "But dancing can lead to immoral behavior!"

"You're exactly right," Jack said. "And the immoral behavior is what we teach is wrong. I would much prefer having my boys dancing in a well-lit and chaperoned gymnasium then in the backseat of a car with a girlfriend."

We taught our sons God's law, "You shall not commit adultery (any sexual activity outside of marriage)." We also taught them why certain behavior was risky and might lead to temptation. But we didn't add to God's law, saying something that God didn't say.

Adam might have told Eve not to touch the tree because he wanted to make sure she did not break the one law God had given.

"'You will not surely die,' the serpent said to the woman" (Genesis 3:4). This was another half-truth from Satan. God said they would die, speaking of both spiritual death and, eventually, physical death. Satan said they would not die, speaking only of immediate physical death.

Satan pointed out the tree of the knowledge of good and evil, describing how wonderful it was and planting seeds of discontent—that Eve and Adam were being deprived of a good thing. He told Eve she could improve this perfect world she was living in. "God knows that when you eat of it your eyes will be opened, and you will be like God, knowing good and evil" (Genesis 3:5).

Satan lied to Eve. Eve listened.

It says that Eve then looked at the forbidden fruit and suddenly saw it in a new light (or should I say *darkness*).

This was a big mistake. She *looked* at something she could not have. Looking at that which we are unable to have brings discontent.

Flesh, Eyes, and Pride

"Well, it's good for food" Eve said. "Food is good. Nothing wrong with eating food. We can eat the fruit on this tree. And even though we can eat off of thousands of other trees and plants, this one has food on it too."

A wife is often the one in charge of feeding her family and making sure they get good, nourishing food. This tree was good for food, and Eve knew the fruit would taste delicious.

So much of the food we get in Africa is starchy. Day after day of rice and potatoes, with maybe a small amount of goat soup, makes you long for fruit. A luscious piece of pineapple, mango, or papaya is often the best part of the meal.

Eve wanted to enjoy the flavor of this particular food as well. This is called the "lust of the flesh."

When we are served our meals in Africa, they usually consist of rice (white), potatoes (white), cabbage (white), matoki (smushed cooked banana, which is white), and ungali (white cornmeal). When a red tomato is added, it makes the plate so much more appetizing.

Maybe this was Eve's thinking—that this fruit, so lovely to look at, would add a nice touch to the dinner plate.

This is called the "lust of the eyes."

Our eyes get us into a lot of trouble. Proverbs 27:20 says, "The eyes of man are never satisfied." And Ecclesiastes 1:8 says, "The eye is not satisfied with seeing."

If you don't believe this, try walking through a mall wearing a blindfold. I don't believe you will be tempted to buy anything (except maybe a cinnamon bun).

It is the eyes that often get women into trouble. We are dissatisfied with the things we see. Our house, our furniture, our clothes, our hair, our kids' clothes, our husband's looks, etc. Our reasoning is simple: we want to improve our surroundings.

Usually none of our other senses are bothered. Our sense of touch doesn't say, "I don't like the way last year's coat feels on my skin." Our ears don't mind if the furniture is old. Our nose doesn't care if we have a bad hair day. Only the eyes—those two little round orbs in your head—cause such discontent. All of us have run into the grocery store for a couple of items and come out with a basketful of groceries.

I believe Satan often uses television today to make us discontented with our surroundings. Maybe this is hinted at in 2 Timothy 3:6 (NASB): "Among them are those who enter into households and captivate weak women weighed down with sins, led on by various impulses."

So Eve looked at the tree. Then she initiated her own kind of understanding. She began to think apart from the Word of God, reasoning, using woman's intuition.

"It looks good," Eve said. "It has a nice color and shape to it. Even though we have more varieties of fruits and vegetables than we could ever eat, this one looks a little better. Nothing wrong with the way it looks."

Women love pretty things, and this fruit was pleasant to look at. It was a nice color and would add a nice touch to the menu.

And then Eve said, "I've been told that if I eat this fruit I will become wise, like God. I know that there is nothing wrong with becoming wise. Wisdom is good. So getting more wisdom from this fruit is good. And if I become more like God, that is good. My goal in life is to become more like God. So this fruit will enable me to become more godly!"

This is called the "boastful pride of life."

Here you have Eve's rationalization and misunderstanding. We all might have thought that she was doing something good—even helpful—but she wasn't. Her motives might have been pure, but they didn't comply with God's Word. The Bible calls this being deceived.

"I am afraid that just as Eve was deceived by the serpent's cunning (NASB: "craftiness"), your minds may somehow be led astray from your sincere and pure devotion to Christ" (2 Corinthians 11:3).

In I Timothy 2:14 we are told, "It was not Adam who was deceived, but the woman being deceived, fell into transgression" (NASB).

Eve was trusting in her own ability to reason things out, in contrast to the wisdom reflected in Proverbs 3:5-7:

> "Trust in the Lord with all your heart,
>   And do not lean on your own understanding.
> In all your ways acknowledge Him,
>   And He will make your paths straight.
> Do not be wise in your own eyes;
>   Fear the Lord and turn away from evil."

Eve was being wise in her own eyes. She was leaning on her own understanding.

She believed she was being helpful, wise, and discerning. So she ate the fruit. Then she gave it to Adam.

Adam Listens to Eve

Now God had given Adam the law directly. He knew the rules. Upon condition of his perfect, personal, and continued obedience, Adam was sure of eternal paradise for himself and his heirs forever. And Adam stood as the father and representative of all mankind.

Even in this perfect setting, God wanted Adam to understand authority and the threat of dreadful consequences of disobedience. This was clearly defined before Eve was created.

There's disagreement and confusion about what Adam was doing while the serpent was tempting Eve. Was he there the whole time? Did he come in the middle of the conversation? Did he watch Eve pick the fruit? Or did Eve give the fruit to him when he showed up after she ate it? We are not really told how the scenario unfolded. But we do know how the story ended.

When Eve gave Adam the fruit, he should have put his arm around her, said that he understood her reasoning and her desire to be helpful, but that he couldn't eat the fruit because God had said not to.

Maybe Adam did say that to Eve, but Eve's feminine logic, understanding, and influence persuaded Adam to sin. A wife has tremendous power over her husband. She has the power to make her husband glad he walked in the door after work or sorry he came home—just by the way she greets him.

Eve was able to get Adam to listen to her. Adam knew what God had said. God had spoken directly to Adam, *commanded* him. But Adam listened to his wife, and it plunged mankind into spiritual darkness.

Adam was put on trial, and he failed.

He knew the rules, but he disobeyed. And Man still has an aversion to being restrained from anything forbidden.

We're told in Romans 5:12, "Through one man sin entered into the world, and death through sin, and so death spread to all men, because all sinned."

Eve was deceived, because she thought she was being helpful, but Adam sinned willfully.

As soon as the two of them ate the fruit, they knew they had disobeyed God. Now they had this powerful sense of guilt that made them want to hide from Him. Their sin had separated them from God. They were still naked, but now they were ashamed.

So they painstakingly sewed fig leaves together to try to make themselves presentable to God, to hide their shame and to be acceptable before a holy God. That must have been a very hard and difficult task, taking a bunch of leaves that would crack and tear to make coverings for their bodies.

Right there was the beginning of religious good works—trying to do something in our own strength to make ourselves acceptable before a holy God. But it didn't work then, and it doesn't work now.

God said to Adam, "Because you listened to your wife and ate from the tree about which I commanded you, 'You must not eat of it,' cursed is the ground because of you. Through painful toil you will eat of it all the days of your life" (Genesis 3:17).

This might be the reason why husbands are often hesitant to receive advice from their wives. But the lesson we learn from this story is that it is not listening to God that brings disaster.

Jeremiah 6:19 says, "Hear, O earth: behold, I am bringing disaster on this people, the fruit of their plans, because they have not listened to My words" (NASB).

In Mark 4:24, Jesus said, "Take care what you listen to" (NASB).

Today, women look around and see the mess we are in and want to change it. They want to improve our world. Their motives may be pure. But who are they listening to?

Apart from an understanding of biblical principles, the changes women make will only serve to increase the problems we now find in our society.

If we aren't listening to God and His Word, and instead are listening to the world, the flesh, and the devil, we will continue to bring disaster to our society.

Just Like Eve

I used to think that if I had been in the Garden of Eden, I wouldn't have done what Eve did. I could have overlooked that one little forbidden fruit. But I do it daily!

Daily I'm deceived, thinking that my ways, my intuition, my understanding, my ideas, and my feelings are the best way to go.

Daily I love the world and the things in the world more than I love God.

Just like Eve.

In 1 John 2:15-16 we're told, "Do not love the world, nor the things in the world. If anyone loves the world, the love of the Father is not in him. For all that is in the world, the lust of the flesh and the lust of the eyes and the boastful pride of life, is not from the Father, but is from the world" (NASB).

Notice what it says here and its parallel in Genesis 3:6:

- "the lust of the flesh"   → "good for food."
- "the lust of the eyes"   → "delight to the eyes"
- "the boastful pride of life" → "desirable to make one wise."

We're told that this "is not from the Father, but is from the world." And 2 Corinthians 4:4 says that Satan is the god of this world, and that he "has blinded the minds of the unbelieving, that they might not see the light of the gospel of the glory of Christ."

I can understand why unbelieving women today reject God's Word.

But Satan is also at work deceiving you and me, so that we will reject God's Word and replace it with our own understanding.

In Colossians 2:4, Paul pleads that "no one may deceive you with persuasive or fine-sounding arguments."

Do you believe you are not being deceived?

Being deceived is so subtle—its very meaning implies that we don't know when it's happening. Satan, the "god of this world," would substitute God's ways with his ways, which appeal to our fallen nature and thus make more sense to us and seem more logical and rational.

And women in the church today are falling for it—hook, line, and sinker.

Women today are saying: "I want things. More things will make me happy. A new house, new furniture, a new job, maybe a new husband. I look around and see other people with a lot more than I have, and it's not fair." Isn't that the lust of the eyes?

Women today are also saying: "I want my way. I have needs too. Why should I be the one to take care of others when I'm so needy myself? I don't want to spend my life being a slave. I don't need anyone else to look after. And besides, the feeling just isn't there anymore. I must look out for number one." Isn't that the lust of the flesh?

And women around the world are saying: "God's Word is old-fashioned and outdated. This is a new millennium. All this talk about submission and domesticity is for the dark ages. I'm liberated. I'm educated. I have good ideas about what I should or shouldn't do, and the Bible doesn't match up. And meeting the needs of my husband definitely won't bring me fulfillment." Isn't that the pride of life?

So you see, the thinking of women today isn't really new. It's as old as the fall.

Resist the Devil

The Bible calls this the activity of Satan, "a deluding influence so that they might believe what is false" (2 Thessalonians 2:11).

Today the world is full of "deluding influences" that would lead us astray. They are called deluding because they seem good and right.

But listen to 2 Corinthians 11:14-15: "Satan disguises himself as an angel of light. Therefore it is not surprising if his servants also disguise themselves as servants of righteousness" (NASB).

There are influences out there that seem good, but are destroying our relationships and our society.

John pleads in 1 John 3:7: "Little children, let no one deceive you" (RSV). I was deceived. I was leaning on my own understanding and was wise in my own eyes. I didn't believe the truth of Scripture, that it would bring me fulfillment or happiness.

And I'm discovering that I am not alone.

It stands to reason that if the god of this world is the father of lies, the great deceiver, and that the whole world lies in the lap of the wicked one (according to 1 John 5:19), then the women of today will be deceived when it comes to their design and role as women.

Either we will embrace our role, our helper design, our purpose, or we will resent it.

"Let no one deceive you with empty words, for because of these things the wrath of God comes upon the sons of disobedience" (Ephesians 5:6, NASB).

God calls the philosophy of the world "empty words." They have no substance to provide a foundation to our society and to future generations. And our relationships today will affect our children and our children's children.

"Progressive" Parents?

As I briefly explained at the beginning of the book, I came from an unusual family—one that had been promoting women's liberation and the sexual revolution since the beginning of the twentieth century. I am quite familiar with the world's message concerning what will make women happy.

I had parents who were married for sixty-five years, but were very liberal, very progressive. They gave each other permission to have affairs, and yet they were devoted to one another throughout their long lives. I never heard my mother and father raise their voices with each other, and rarely did they have a disagreement. I think they were just so compatible that they let the other one do whatever he or she wanted, no questions asked.

I never heard the phrase "a wife should submit to her husband," but my mother gave me the impression that my father came first in her life, even though she was a well-educated, liberal-thinking woman. Both she and her mother were college graduates back when that wasn't so common for women.

My mother graduated with a master's degree in French from UCLA, and then she went to Columbia University in New York and got a nursing degree while training at Presbyterian Hospital. Her father, a family doctor, attended medical school at the University of Pennsylvania and Johns Hopkins. He was one of the founders of the Hollywood Bowl. He and my grandmother hosted famous lecturers for many years in their Hollywood home, early twentieth-century intellectual leaders such as the famous athiest Bertrand Russell, Margaret Sanger (the abortion and birth control advocate), Bolshevik activist Emma Goldman, author Upton Sinclair, and Clarence and Ruby Darrow, two of their closest friends.

My father was shuffled between parents most of his early life, and attended sixteen different elementary schools. When it came time to go to high school, he vowed to stay in one school, but that meant he had to walk a mile, travel on two streetcars, and take a bus to get to school—two hours each way. But he graduated with honors and went on to earn three master's degrees in engineering at Cal Tech. To me it proved nature over nurture.

I'm the youngest of three girls and totally different than my sisters. My mother use to say, "Well you're different because you were a breech baby and you came out backwards."

I thought about that a lot, because most everything my sisters loved to do, I didn't. They were artists that loved to do art. I loved to color in coloring books, and they told me that coloring books were the worst thing in the world for young people. They loved horses and bought their own as young teenagers and went horseback riding all the time. I wanted to stay home and play with paper dolls. They were not interested in clothes, and I wanted new clothes all the time. They went off to art schools during the pre-beatnik, pre-hippie movement. I was a Gamma Phi Beta sorority girl, keeping up with all the latest styles and trends. In every area I was totally different.

My family held to the position that religions, particularly Christianity and missionaries, had done more harm than good in the world. My father and I would have deep discussions about the expanding universe—where it was going, where it came from, how long it would last—and the concept of God never entered the conversation. Growing up, my "god" was Mother Nature, and the protection of the environment was a driving force in my family. I remember one member of my family getting angry because Jesus said that humans were worth more than sparrows.

One time I called my mother on her seventieth birthday to wish her a happy birthday, and my dad said she was out marching for nuclear peace and to call back later. They were part of an organization promoting one-world government. They conserved energy, they conserved water, and when they heard that dolphins were being caught in tuna nets, they stopped eating tuna. Whatever they could do on their own personal level, they tried to do. They were staunch, committed environmentalists, and together they practiced what they preached, and were both very involved in political action. My father was an activist until he died at the age of ninety-six.

I admired my mother and father and loved them very much. They taught me so many lessons, were kind and hospitable, and were never judgmental. I owe a lot to them.

I was taught at an early age that it's better to just do your own thing and try to be kind and gracious to people in the world and not even think about God. I put the stories in the Bible right there alongside fairy tales and the Easter Bunny. I thought that was pretty much the thinking of all my relatives and their friends.

I understand now that I was greatly transformed by a gracious work of God in my life. Romans 12:2 urges us not to be conformed to this world, but to be "transformed by the renewing of your mind." This transformation can only take place when we listen to God's Word, rather than the world—even when His Word seems to contradict our rational, logical, reasoning mind.

Eve was convinced she was doing something good and right. Women today are convinced as well. But if we aren't listening to God's Word—and to God's people speaking God's Word—then as a result we will be deceived. So we need to be listening to God's Word ourselves and then speaking God's Word in order to encourage other women.

I pray that we will be women who understand why we were created, our purpose and our design. I pray that we will understand the importance of an intimate relationship with God first and then with others. The Bible tells us to "Love the Lord your God with all your heart and with all your soul and with all your mind. This is the first and greatest commandment. And the second is like it: 'Love your neighbor as yourself'" (Matthew 22:37-39).

Finally, I pray that we will understand that if we are married, our closest "neighbor" is our husband.

CHAPTER 14

The Holy Spirit as Helper

I NEVER LIKED the term "helpmate" when it came to my role as a wife. To me it seemed subservient, like a servant or even a slave. I thought it was like the kitchen help, and it seemed very demeaning.

I also didn't like it because I knew that husbands were so needy. They are constantly asking for help to do this or that, and even though most women want to help, we resent *having* to be helpers. We want to help make our home a better place, our community a better place, even the world a better place. But for some reason we don't have that same desire to make our husband a better husband and help him. I think part of the reason is because of the whole dynamic of our worldly thinking.

But we are created to be helpers, and somewhere along the line God impressed upon me the value of that ministry.

There is someone else called the Helper: the Holy Spirit. "I will ask the Father, and He will give you another Helper, that He may be with you forever" (John 14:16, NASB).

The role of woman is in many ways similar to the role of the Holy Spirit.

Let's look at some of these similarities.

The Holy Spirit is the life-giver, who brings new birth: "Unless one is born of water and the Spirit he cannot enter into the kingdom of God" (John 3:5). Women are the ones who bring forth new life and give birth. (The name "Eve" literally means "life-giver.")

The Holy Spirit is also called the "Comforter" (John 14:16, KJV). Women are imbued with the ability to comfort and encourage as part of their role.

The Holy Spirit is grieved when we sin (Ephesians 4:30). Women, in particular, grieve when things are not going well in a family.

The Holy Spirit helps our weakness (Romans 8:26). Women are most often the helpers whenever and wherever there are needs, both in and outside the home.

The Holy Spirit intercedes for us on our behalf before the Father (Romans 8:27). A wife pleads the needs of her children to their father.

The Holy Spirit reminds us of those things we need to remember: "The Helper, the Holy Spirit, whom the Father will send in my name, He will teach you all things, and bring to your remembrance all that I said to you" (John 14:26, NASB). Women are usually the ones who remind members of the family of those things they have forgotten, whether it's a birthday or anniversary, or where to find the socks and car keys.

The Holy Spirit does not speak on His own behalf, but represents the Father to us, His children, and says what the Father wants Him to say. "When He, the Spirit of truth, comes, He will guide you into all the truth, for He will not speak on His own initiative, but whatever He hears, He will speak" (John 16:13, NASB). A wife speaks to her children those things that their father wishes them to know.

The Holy Spirit gives honor and glory to the Father, not to Himself (John 16:14). A wife is to honor and respect her husband as head of the home.

The Holy Spirit is equal with the Father, truly God, with all the qualities, characteristics, abilities, and attributes of God Almighty. But the Holy Spirit exercises a different role, different than the Father and the Son.

Woman is equal with the man, but fulfills a different role: "There is neither Jew nor Greek, there is neither slave nor free man, there is neither male nor female, for you are all one in Christ Jesus" (Galatians 3:28).

Just as the Holy Spirit has a ministry different than those of the Father and the Son, wives also have a ministry different than that of their husbands within marriage. It is not a lesser role, but it is a different role. And just as the ministry of the Holy Spirit as Helper is vitally important, so is the role of wife as helper to her husband.

When Jesus was leaving his disciples behind before His ascension, he promised to send the Holy Spirit to them (John 16:7). In fact, He told them that it was to their advantage that He left them, "for if I do not go away, the Helper will not come to you; but if I go, I will send Him to you."

After Jesus ascended into heaven, it was one week before the Holy Spirit came down to the waiting followers of Christ. When Jesus said to the Holy Spirit that He was now to go down to earth and be the Helper to His people, what if the Holy Spirit had replied, "What! You want *me* to go help *them*? They are so needy. So sinful. They take us for granted. They are often disobedient, rebellious, and so ungrateful. They don't believe your words. They don't talk to you as much as they should. And they don't seem to improve much. They are not worthy of my help, love, care, or concern. Are you sure you want me to be their helper?"

But the Holy Spirit did not say that. He was willing to come and fulfill His role as our Helper even though we were not worthy, because that is who He is. That is His design. That is His ministry and role.

Today women are looking at their husbands and saying, "God, do you really want me to help him? He's so needy. So sinful. So ungrateful. He takes me for granted. He hardly speaks to me. He's not worthy of my help, love, care, or concern. Are you sure you want me to be his helper?"

We are to be a helper to our husband, not because he is worthy, but because that is our role, that is our ministry. It is who we are, our Creator's design. We are equals in the marriage, but our function is different—we are the helpers.

I hear women say, "Who needs men? They aren't worth the trouble!" But the issue is, "men need women!" It is our challenge, and we must have the courage to accept it.

When we carry out our role, we will begin to experience the fulfillment that God created us for. Not because our husbands are worthy, but because God is worthy, and it is His design, His will, His purpose for us. Whether we are married or not, God has created us to be helpers to a needy world. But if we *are* married, our *first* ministry is to help meet the needs of our husband.

Identifying the Enemies

I don't know about you, but I do not always want to help others that often, and I am certainly not excited about being a "helpmate." I think most wives feel the same way. But we cannot base our faith on feelings. It must be based on God's Word. It cannot be based on what society or culture says, but on the truth of Scripture. It cannot be based on what the world is saying, because the world is not speaking truth. It cannot be based on what our own heart is telling us, because our hearts are "de-

THE HOLY SPIRIT AS HELPER

ceitfully wicked." And we cannot base our feelings on what the devil tells us, for he is the father of lies. These are all enemies, according to the Bible, and cannot be trusted.

This is a constant struggle, common to all followers of Christ. It is normal, universal, and part of being a child of God. God speaks much about this struggle in His Word. Words like enemy, hostility, fight, warfare, battle, and suffering are found throughout the Bible.

What are some enemies in our life?

Lack of submission, selfishness, unforgiveness, resentment, bitterness, unkindness, bickering, nagging, ungratefulness—these are all enemies of the flesh—as well as fleshly desires, immorality, jealousy, lust, and self-pity.

It is no wonder that we get weary, tired, discouraged, and defeated. These enemies are really out to get us, to destroy us, to make us ineffective as wives.

I believe weak marriages have done more to destroy our country, harm the testimony of Christ, and hurt our children than humanism, legalism, materialism, pantheism, or communism. Strong, healthy marriages will do more to reach the world for Christ than any correctly orthodox message in a strained relationship.

Our culture, and especially our children, desperately need to see that God is real, that Scripture is true, and that biblical principles work. If our marriages aren't healthy and strong, if husbands and wives are not committed to long-term relationships that persevere "for better or worse," what kind of message are we giving our culture, our society, and our kids about what it means to follow Christ?

The easiest place to be a "Christian" is in church, among friends, listening to sermons, singing, being nice, and looking good. But home, behind closed doors, is where "the rubber meets the road." It is here where our marriage is lived out for our children to see, and where the relationship is in the crucible.

The Bible says that marriage brings many troubles in this life (1 Corinthians 7:28), but God doesn't expect us to flee the marriage because we have problems. He has told us that in this world we will have tribulation, but that He will never leave us nor forsake us. We can find the ability to persevere in the difficult times because we can do all things through Christ who strengthens us (Philippians 4:13).

To deny God's power to work in relationships is to deny God, and Psalm 53:1 says that if we say there is no God, we are fools and "have committed abominable injustice" (NASB).

"The fool has said in his heart, 'There is no God'" (Psalm 14:1). I didn't believe that God could work in my situation, and He called me a fool.

The Bible tells us that whoever denies Jesus is the Christ, the Redeemer, is a liar! (1 John 2:22). Christ came to redeem relationships. If we deny His ability to do this, God calls us liars.

Marriages today are in trouble. This is true wherever I go throughout the world. I've had the opportunity to speak to hundreds of wives on every continent, and many are hurting, discouraged, unhappy, and scared. The first time I spoke to African women, I thought I wouldn't be able to relate to women from a different culture, but I soon learned that women are the same all over the world—with the same struggles, worries, problems, and needs. And we all have some of the same goals and desires—to have good marriages and strong, healthy families.

Even Christian marriages are in a mess. They are poor testimonies to the world, to local churches, and especially to the children in these marriages. We have a wonderful opportunity to be "salt and light" to a needy world by showing what good marriages look like.

The world is in desperate need of role models, and should be able to look to the church to see what God can do in the lives of His people, who trust Him and call Him "Father." Our children should want to grow up to be just like Mom and Dad, to have a marriage like their parents, and to love and follow their God.

Where did we go wrong? What has caused so many marriages to crack, crumble, or fall apart completely? Why are there so few role models of biblical relationships?

According to Titus 2:5, the older, mature Christian women are to help train the younger women "how to love their husbands." I wish there had been an older woman like that in my life when I was a young wife.

The church and marriage are the two institutions God has ordained. So we know that these two institutions will be under attack from the enemy. And that attack often begins with the wife, just as it did back in the garden of Eden.

I like to tell a story to the couples in Africa when we teach on marriage:

> God says to every women in the world, "Take all your husband's sins, problems, weaknesses, and shortcomings, and put them in a big paper bag. Close it up and bring it to me."
>
> Then God takes every bag and puts them all in a huge pile. When all the bags are gathered, He says to each woman, "Now you can go and look into each bag and take home anyone you want to be your new husband."
>
> The first woman goes up to the pile, picks out a paper bag, opens it up, and looks inside. "Oooooh, not that one." And she quickly closes it up and puts in back. She takes another one, looks inside, and says, "Oh no! Not that one either!" She opens the next one. "Yuck!" She takes another, and another, and another. The reaction is the same: "There's no way I could live with that one."
>
> After each woman has looked in every bag, she ends up taking her own bag home with her! She realizes that everyone in the world has problems. The ones we are familiar with are easier to live with. We think the grass is greener on the other side of the fence, but it's just as hard to mow.

When I tell that story in Africa, both the men and women cheer and applaud, because they can identify with those feelings, and yet they want to have strong, lasting marriages. They want to know how to do it, and they are willing to do what it takes to keep their marriages together. In a way, they are more committed to marriages than Americans. There is not much divorce because hardship, suffering, and trouble are a normal part of life. They have had to learn to be content in trials and difficult circumstances, which helps them cope in marriage. It's just that they often do not have a lot of understanding of biblical principles. But they want to learn and will apply whatever biblical teaching they receive.

The women are confused by the concept of submission, because the empowerment of women is pushed throughout Africa. When I would teach on submission to husbands, I would tell them, "You could be President of Uganda and rule over all the men and women in the county and be their leader, but when you go home at night, you are to be in submission to your own husband. He's the head of your home and of your family and of your marriage."

And it would be like a light bulb switching on, because they would understand that there is a need for leadership in the home. Jack would teach the men how they were to love their wives as Christ loved the church and be an example of sacrificial love. He would tell them, "If you treat your wife like a queen, she will treat you like a king."

African women are very teachable, but many of them have messed up lives, which makes it very difficult for them. Even Solomon couldn't answer some of their questions: "What do you do when you have a husband who's unfaithful and then comes home with AIDS?" or "What do you do when your husband has two or three other wives and you are the only believer?" or "What do you do when you were circumcised as a young girl so you have no sexual pleasure, but you want to be able to please your husband?" Their sad situations are heartbreaking, but they still have the desire to keep their marriages intact.

As I look around, I see many baby boomers with gray heads. What a wealth of encouragement and influence they can be—they should be—to the younger women in our culture who are not hearing what God says about their role.

Let me repeat Titus 2:3-4: "Older women are to . . . teach what is good, that they may encourage the young women to love their husbands, to love their children, to be sensible, pure, workers at home, kind, being subject to their own husbands, that the Word of God may not be dishonored."

My guess is that no woman who is reading this book would deliberately want to dishonor God's Word, but this verse says we dishonor God's Word when we refuse to follow God's plan for women.

ALL OF US want to serve God and do His will, but much of the time we are deceived.

As I think about being a helper to my husband, I am reminded of a story my friend Nancy told me. Her little girl came into the kitchen and saw her making cookies. Her daughter said, "Mommy, I want to help you!"

Nancy said, "You want to help me?"

"Oh, yes, Mommy, I want to help!"

Nancy repeated, "You really want to help me? Then please go into the living room and pick up all your toys."

Her daughter replied, "Oh, no, Mommy! I want to help you make *cookies!*"

I was like that little girl. I wanted to help God, serve God, minister for God, be intimate with God, be an obedient child of God. But I wanted to "make cookies" when God was saying to me, "Carol, if you really want to serve me, then go and be a helper to your husband!" But I wanted to serve God on my terms and in my way, not necessarily on His terms, in accordance with what His will was for me.

Let us be biblical women, authentic and genuine, true to God, true to His Word, true to our calling, and true to our helper design.

You will rejoice. Your husband will rejoice. The church will rejoice. And God will be glorified.

Part IV

Helpful Hints on Marriage

CHAPTER 15

Hints for a Successful Marriage

IN THIS PART of the book I will outline some of the things we found helpful during the course of our marriage. This chapter provides some general hints for married couples, and the following chapters list some tips that are particularly beneficial to husbands, as well as a list of Scripture verses to help "light the way" for couples who desire to see God work in their marriages.

These are not meant to be viewed simply as a "to do" list. They represent a summary of the ways God taught us over the years. Some of these principles were learned (and relearned) through many hardships and painful struggles, as the earlier part of this book describes. I would also reinforce that it is God alone who accomplishes in us this work of becoming like Him, and we are powerless to do it on our own. Thus the teaching in this section will prove to be helpful to you only if you approach it with a simple, childlike faith, depending completely on the One "who works in you to will and to do what pleases Him" (Philippians 2:13).

1. Be committed to the authority of Scripture.

Our relationship was founded on the Word of God, and that, more than any other thing, kept us together in our marriage. When we made vows before God to stay together "till death do us part" and to be faithful to one another, we knew it was binding. We knew that to go against God's laws was sin. It was being obedient to those laws that was the hard part. (Chapter 17, "Helpful Verses," lists some Bible passages we found to be particularly helpful.)

2. Believe that you are partners in ministry.

My first model of ministry was Bill and Vonette Bright. They worked as a team, as do all the couples on Crusade staff, even to this day. They planned, prayed, and organized together. Vonette met with me regularly, to go over the memory verses she would give me, encouraged me, and prayed with me. I met with other sorority girls in her home (they were living with author Henrietta Mears) across the street from UCLA, where we would study the Bible together and talk about our new faith in Christ.

Seminary professors' wives also showed me the importance of partnering with your husband, whatever his calling might be. Whether actively involved in his work, or working behind the scenes, try to provide the support and encouragement he needs to be the best husband, father, provider, and leader he can be.

3. Recognize your differences and be willing to complement each other.

Jack and I were so different. (See our list of "opposites" in Chapter 12.) For example, he was always on time; I was pretty laid back about what time it was and therefore was usually late to everything. I learn directions quickly, have an internal compass so I always know "which way is north" and study maps. Jack had trouble returning home even after a year of living someplace. Early on, these differences were a source of much friction, as I wanted Jack to be like me, and he wanted me to be like him.

Then we realized that these differences were why God put us together. I needed Jack to help me learn to be diligent when it came to time, and he needed to learn to relax and not live by the clock. I am a procrastinator, doing everything last minute. He was a list-maker and did everything today, even if it could be put off until tomorrow. I helped him become more laid back, and he helped me put my responsibilities in order. I sure miss his urging and prodding not to put off doing things that need to get done.

We got to the point where we expected to think completely different, and laughed every time we discovered a new "opposite." Together we were able to do so much more than each one separately—which is what marriage is all about: "one flesh."

4. Help each other out in your duties and ministries.

Early in our marriage, our duties were hard and fast. I took care of the kids, managed the home, kept up with anniversaries and birthdays, communicated with the in-laws, etc. Jack studied and pastored.

But it wasn't long before Jack needed help in his ministry. The small church he planted didn't have a secretary, so I started typing up his sermons. Then there were letters to send, people to visit, nurseries to set up, and women to organize. He couldn't do it all, but I couldn't do all those things and everything else I was supposed to do either.

We learned the value of saying, "What can I do to help?" It didn't matter if it was my duty or his responsibility. He often washed the dishes and cleaned the kitchen, and he became the one who did all the vacuuming and mopping of the floors, which was a huge help to me. If it was within our ability to help, we pretty much tried to do it.

5. Pray together, but don't necessarily have "devotions" together.

Jack and I had spent many hours learning biblical truths together before we were married. I thought this would continue throughout our years together. But it wasn't long before several things happened. Jack's interests and mine were on two different levels, and our spiritual needs were not the same. Jack was learning deep spiritual truths as a seminary student. I was just trying to get through the day as a new wife, new employee, and before long, a new mother. I needed a time alone, a "quiet time," where I could have my space to learn and grow at my own pace.

Jack and I fully intended to study the Bible together. Soon after we were married, after supper, we started to sit down and read, beginning in Genesis. We had not gone beyond Genesis 6 before I started asking questions about creation, marriage, and the causes of the flood. Before long, we would be debating—I called it "discussion," but Jack called it "arguing." So we decided the best thing for us was to have our devotions separately and save our "discussions" for another time.

But whether you have devotions together or not, it is still important that you pray together regularly. It will remind you daily that you are both completely dependent upon God and His grace, that you are both equal before God—and equally important to Him—and that he is the source of your "oneness" as a couple. Jack and I did not always pray together during our difficult years, but later in life we would usually pray together about three times a week for an hour.

6. Don't stifle creativity or interests.

Jack loved sports. He was a PE major in college and had planned to be a coach or teach athletics before his call to ministry. Although his ability to play diminished as he got older, his interest in sports never left him. When the boys were young, he coached them in football and basketball. As an adult he played in tennis tournaments.

On the other hand, I liked crafts. I spent a lot of spare time sewing, knitting, quilting, making stuff. When we were able to remodel the basement into a bedroom, I turned the extra room upstairs into a workroom (often called the "junk room") so I would have a place to do all my projects and close the door.

7. **Recognize whether you or your spouse is better at handling money.**

I love to do bookkeeping. It's like working a puzzle (one of my favorite things to do) when I put all the numbers where they should be, balance the checkbook, and figure out the budget. Jack was glad to have me take care of the finances, pay the bills, and write out the tithe checks, because I was better at it than he was.

8. **Don't be possessive or jealous of your spouse's outside friends.**

Whether it was sporting events or baby showers, Jack and I attended many functions alone. We went out with our own friends, and I would take weekend trips with other women.

9. **Don't be a child-centered family.**

We have been around parents that let the children make the decisions and rule the roost. Of course, we considered our kids' preferences and desires, but when it came to making decisions, we didn't let their whining and crying influence us.

10. **Have a weekly "Family Night" with your children.**

Jack's position as a pastor could have consumed all his time if he had let it. Meetings, visitation, sick calls, counseling, studying, and services demanded his time and attention.

Except for emergencies, like a death or accident, we reserved Friday night for the family. Jack would write it on his Daytimer, and when someone asked him to do something that night, he would tell them, "I'm sorry, but I already have something on my calendar for that night. Can we meet the next day?"

Even though he was busy every night of the week, the boys knew that when Friday came, he would be spending the evening with them. They were content with that. I've discovered that a busy schedule doesn't hurt children, but a bitter or resentful attitude about the busy schedule is what destroys a family.

11. Make arrangements to get away from your children to do adult things, alone or with other adults.

One of the reasons we organized so many church functions for the adults was so the couples in our church could enjoy an evening away from parenting. There is a different dynamic when children are around. Sometimes our kids would ask why they could not come with us, and we would explain to them how important it was for Mom and Dad to get away by ourselves, that it made our marriage better. They were happy to hear that, and I know it made them feel more secure.

We organized a lot of parties at the church for the adults. We told the children when they would complain, "This is one of the advantages of being grown up!" Potlucks, Valentine banquets, and Halloween parties were favorites among the people. Jack and I loved to disguise ourselves at the Halloween parties. One year we were Indians, wrapped in blankets. Another year we went as Arabs.

12. Cultivate friendships with other couples who uplift you.

This was probably one of the greatest ways God preserved our marriage. When we were with other couples, having a good time, telling stories, laughing and enjoying meaningful discussions, it created an atmosphere that enabled me to see Jack in a different light. I watched other people take pleasure in his company, and admire and respect him.

Bob and Sunny were good friends with whom we played bridge and took beach trips. They were fun, and they wanted to be around me and Jack. It made me realize that many of the problems I was having with Jack stemmed from my own bad attitude, and not because he was truly the jerk I thought he was.

13. Date at least once a month.

We didn't do this until late in our marriage, but we should have. It might have saved me from years of negative thinking if Jack and I had cultivated some fun times—just the two of us.

14. Never keep a list of each other's wrongs or hold grudges.

Jack and I both had terrible memories when it came to remembering what the other person had done. There were times when Jack did something wrong and I would say to myself,—"I'm going to remember this, so the next time I do something wrong I can remind him of his faults." But I would forget when we would get into an argument.

Jack could blow up at something stupid I said or did, but ten minutes later act like it had never happened. I had a tendency to bottle my feelings up and keep quiet.

One example was when our boys were little and it seemed like the trash can in the kitchen was always full. It would be overflowing, and Jack would walk right by. It made me angry. He would ask me, "What's wrong?" and I would reply, "Nothing." Then he would drag it out of me. "The trash can is overflowing. Can't you see? It needs to be emptied!" His response: "I'll be happy to empty the trash. Just ask me! I'm not a mind reader." But I wanted him to be a mind reader. I didn't want to have to ask him. I wanted him to see it. But I wanted something that would rarely happen.

15. Learn to say how you really feel when you are hurt or angry.

I've explained how we were taught at Marble Retreat to be honest about our feelings instead of beating around the bush (see pages 79-80). A straightforward approach to feelings can prevent many an argument.

16. Don't let "big fights" scare you. Often they can be very productive.

We didn't scream and yell, hit or bite! But when we were completely at odds with each other, we continued to hang in there until it was resolved. Our children saw us disagree and yet stay committed, which has helped them in their marriages.

17. Don't criticize each other's parents.

It was alright for me to call my parents "80-year-old California hippies," because they were. I often told stories about their idiosyncrasies and weird ways. But when Jack made fun of them, it hurt! This went both ways, and we realized that certain issues were off-limits, and that criticizing and making fun of each other's parents was "hitting below the belt."

18. Recognize that you act differently around parents.

When I went home to my parents' house, I wanted to be "Daddy's little girl" again. I became their daughter, and acted like I was back in their family, telling stories of my childhood and reminiscing. I didn't want to be a wife, which was a harder role. Jack learned to take a stack of books to read when we visited my folks in their cabin in the woods of Marin County, north of San Francisco.

When we visited his folks, I sat back and marveled at the way they did things. We both thought our families were strange, but we loved them very much.

**19. Try to maintain a sense of humor, and don't take
yourselves too seriously—we are fallen creatures.**

Jack and I enjoyed jokes and pranks. We often would tell
funny stories about each other, and usually the teasing was
fun. I tried to learn later in our marriage not to let the kidding
degenerate into hurtful ridicule.

**20. Be sensitive to each other's physical weaknesses and
moody days.**

When I learned that Jack had low blood sugar if he didn't
eat, I made sure he didn't go hungry. It was amazing to see the
difference in his demeanor when he had food! Sometimes it
would irritate me that he couldn't control his emotions when
he was hungry, but I had to realize that God made him that way,
and I had to show compassion.

**21. Allow each other to have a certain amount of discretionary
money to spend.**

I hated being accountable to Jack for every dime I spent.
I had pet projects that I wanted to spend money on. Sometimes
I would ask him, but often I would spend money without telling
him.

Our marriage counselor discovered that this had been a
problem, so he suggested a solution. "Each month, give Carol a
certain amount of money that she can use as she wishes. She can
save it, spend it, or give it away—no questions asked."

I thought that was a terrific idea, and it worked. Sometimes
I fudged a little and still gave away extra money, but I knew God
would always provide, which He did.

22. Don't run up credit card debts.

Rarely did we ever pay a finance charge on our credit cards.
They were for emergencies only, and so we did without if the
money wasn't there.

I'm very thankful that we didn't have credit cards at our disposal when we were in seminary. We would have accumulated a lot of debt, and we would have missed out on the blessings of seeing God provide for us in supernatural ways.

When Jack returned to seminary to finish his doctoral program, he was promised some support from the church he had started in California. However, three months after we arrived in Dallas we were told by the church that they were going to give the money to missionaries in New Guinea instead.

There we were, with four little boys under six years old, Jack in the midst of his studies and writing his dissertation, and no income.

Jack had been teaching a class at our church to a large group of couples. Unknown to us, the leader of the class told the group about our unexpected loss of income. He quoted, "A teacher is worthy of his hire," and said if anyone wanted to help us they could send us some money in the mail.

From then on we lived from our mailbox. Just about every day I would find an envelope with money or a check in it. Sometimes a large amount, sometimes just a couple dollars. But for the next fourteen months we paid every bill, never missed a month's rent check, and had enough left over to buy a house-full of furniture when we moved to Roanoke. How sad if we had been able to buy everything we needed on credit cards and had missed that miraculous experience.

23. Solve the "nagging" problem.

I was accused of being "Mrs. Holy Spirit" in my marriage. I thought I had the right ideas about what Jack should do or what he was doing wrong. (This is where the analogy of the wife being a reminder, like the Holy Spirit, goes too far.) I didn't have the faith to believe that the Holy Spirit would convict him of those things, so I nagged him. And he hated it. Jack, like most men, didn't want to hear "advice" from his wife.

During a difficult time in the church, I would try to cheer him up, reminding him of all the good things that were hap-pening, the changed lives, and the people who appreciated his ministry so much. But hearing it from me wasn't enough.

Then one evening he came home and told me that someone in the church had been so encouraging by telling him about all the good things that were happening. "That's exactly what I've been telling you," I said. He replied, "I know. But you're my wife!"

During a discussion—rather, an argument—when I was continuing to nag Jack about something, he asked me why I couldn't just let it go. I told him I did not have the faith to believe God would tell him these things. Then I had an idea.

"What if you give me the names of two men that you really admire and trust, and give me permission to go to them and tell them what I want you to know? Then they can tell you, not me."

He thought about it, and said he would be willing, if it meant that I would stop my nagging. So he gave me two names, elders who were trustworthy and wise.

But an interesting thing happened. Because I wanted to make sure it was really an important issue before I went to them, and therefore prayed about it more fervently, I only went once to one of the men! God seemed to take care of all the other problems that I had seemed so concerned about before.

24. Don't be hesitant to get marriage counseling.

The first time we went to a professional counselor, it was because I thought Jack was the one with problems and that he needed help to make our marriage better.

I soon learned that I was as much, or more, of the problem than he was. It was through counseling that I came to grips with my need to examine myself and see the "beam" in my own eye before criticizing Jack for his "mote."

Counseling gently and efficiently guided me into an understanding of my ministry of marriage and the need to work on myself. There was no "Aha!" moment, but the accumulation of knowledge I gained was invaluable.

"There is wisdom in many counselors."

25. Be more people-oriented than things-oriented. Don't be materialistic.

Some of the most enjoyable times in our marriage were when we had a houseful of people—either for an evening of games or conversation, or houseguests that came for a few days to visit.

I have discovered that the more people-oriented you are, the less you are material-oriented. And people who spend vast amounts of money and time gathering possessions don't seem all that interested in other people. People matter; things don't. And the most important things in life are relationships—with God and others.

CHAPTER 16

Hints for
Husbands

1. You are needy.

It is wise for you to understand that God created you incomplete and with needs. Even though Adam was in a perfect world, with an ideal body, in a wonderful place, with ideal circumstances, it was not enough. God said it wasn't good that man was alone. Man needed more.

It is foolish to think that you don't need your wife. It goes against what God Himself says. It doesn't mean you are inferior or deficient in your abilities. What it means is that God wanted your relationship with your wife to reflect union, oneness, and unselfishness.

Recognizing your needy state makes you realize your dependence upon God's help and creative design to complete you and give you what will meet your needs. It will help you develop a grateful heart and appreciate what God did in meeting those needs by giving you a wife.

2. Your wife is a gift from God.

When God presented to Adam the woman he had designed and fashioned specifically to meet his needs, Adam said, "Wow! This is the one for me!" He realized that God had brought to him a mate who was perfect for him, different from all the thousands of animals and creatures he had finished naming.

God had compassion on Adam's loneliness and met that need, as He meets all our needs. He took deliberate and purposeful care in creating a mate who would complete Adam. Apart from his wife, a husband is crippled and incomplete, with needs that are not being met and deficient abilities.

We are told that a wife is a gift from God (Proverbs 19:14). She is valuable, the crown of her husband, and a good thing (Proverbs 31:10; 12:4; 18:22). She is said to be more precious than rubies and pearls.

How is a costly and valuable gift treated?

When Jack got his first brand new car—not used, not pre-owned, but right from the new car dealer—he was overjoyed. He had never had a new car before. It was a 1963 Rambler American, and it cost less than $1,900.

Jack took such good care of that car. He made sure it stayed clean, both inside and out. He protected it from the elements and installed floor pads and seat coverings. He kept the oil changed and made sure it received the necessary tune-ups. He didn't allow any of the children (three at the time) to eat or drink in the car. He drove it carefully so nobody would run into it. He loved that car.

That is how expensive and valuable cars are treated by most men. Yet God says that your wife is much more valuable, precious, and important than any possession in all the world. She is to be cared for, prized, and loved more than any other gift you could ever hope to receive.

3. You are to love her as Christ loved the church.

Because your wife is such a precious gift, you are to love her. Care for her. Sacrifice for her. God says you are to love her as Christ loved the church and gave Himself for her:

> Husbands, love your wives, just as Christ loved the church and gave himself up for her to make her holy, cleansing her by the washing with water through the word, and to present her to himself as a radiant church, without stain or wrinkle or any other blemish, but holy and blameless.
>
> In this same way, husbands ought to love their wives as their own bodies. He who loves his wife loves himself.
>
> After all, no one ever hated his own body, but he feeds and cares for it, just as Christ does the church—for we are members of his body. 'For this reason a man will leave his father and mother and be united to his wife, and the two will become one flesh.' This is a profound mystery—but I am talking about Christ and the church. However, each one of you also must love his wife as he loves himself. (Ephesians 5:25-33)

Christ did not want to die on the cross. In fact, in the Garden of Gethsemane, Jesus asked His Father to change the whole plan of redemption so that he would not have to go to the cross and give his body to die for the sins of the church. But after asking three times, He finally submitted to the will of the Father and obeyed, because it was the right thing to do.

God is asking husbands to love their wives in the same way— sacrificing, obeying, even when it is hard, because it is the right thing to do, and because it is a picture to the world of what an intimate union involves. Intimacy involves sacrifice, unselfishness, and the forfeiting of rights for the benefit of another.

4. Would you want to submit to you if you were the wife?

Wives are told to be in submission to their own husbands:

> Wives, submit to your husbands as to the Lord. For the husband is the head of the wife as Christ is the head of the church, his body, of which he is the Savior. Now as the church submits to Christ, so also wives should submit to their husbands in everything. (Ephesians 5:22-24)

This is a hard thing to do. We are being told by the world, the flesh, and the devil (all enemies of God) that submission means slavery, subservience, and inferiority. But that is not the case. Biblical submission shows an understanding and appreciation for God's order and creator design.

Women are not inferior. Men and women were created equal in the image of God. We are told there is neither "male nor female, but we are all one in Christ" (Galatians 3:28). A woman could be president of a country and rule over every man, woman, boy, and girl, but when she goes home, she is to be in submission "to her own husband."

But even though it is a command from God, it is very difficult for a wife to do, because we want to be in charge of our own lives and not be in submission to anyone.

A husband who loves his wife as Christ loves the church will make it easier for his wife to submit, by being a loving leader, listening to her, and giving her the opportunity to make her opinions known. A wise husband will know that his wife is smarter in many areas and has an understanding of the home and family that he does not have, and therefore will listen to her. Most of the time there will be agreement and consensus.

In those rare times when there is no meeting of the minds, then the husband is the final authority. But that authority is to be one of gentleness, love, and compassion, as Christ shows to us when we want to go astray.

Treating your wife the way you want to be treated, showing mercy, love, and compassion, will make it easier for her to submit to you, respond to you, and meet your needs in return.

5. Help your wife if you want her to respond to you.

God made women to be the responders. Men are the initiators. Wives react to the treatment they receive.

Men respond sexually to just the sight of a beautiful woman. But women respond to the treatment and loving actions of their husbands. It's been said, "Men give affection to get sex; women give sex to get affection." A wise husband will give his wife affection, hugging her with no ulterior motives, telling her "I love you," but also showing it by his actions.

Women give their bodies all day long to take care of the needs of the family. They carry babies for nine months in their body, they nurse the babies, they lose sleep, they drag their bodies out of bed to care for the needs of the family. They use their bodies to wash clothes, clean the house, buy groceries, cook meals, do the dishes, and put the kids to bed. Many go to work every day to help earn money. Then their husbands also want them to give their bodies to them at night. They are tired! They are the weaker partner (1 Peter 3:7).

If you want your wife to respond physically to you, then help her out. Do whatever is necessary to keep her from becoming so tired that she has nothing left for you at the end of the day. One wife said, "For me, sex begins in the kitchen. If my husband helps me with the dishes, I'm more likely to respond to him."

Most women are willing to work hard if they know their husband is working hard also. But when the wife is doing chores around the house while the husband sits and watches TV, he should not be surprised when she doesn't respond very well to his advances.

A little help goes a long way. When I got pregnant after three months of marriage, I continued working while Jack was attending seminary. I had morning sickness, I was working five and a half days a week, and I disliked housework, so our apartment often looked like a calamity. Once in a while Jack would say, "Let me help you clean up," and he would pick up a sock or two. That was all the support I needed to continue cleaning up the rest of the place.

It is the attitude of helping that encourages a wife to meet the needs of her husband, which she knows is God's will but is still a difficult challenge.

6. Take care of your body.

Men like an attractive wife. They feel proud to have a lovely woman on their arm. They appreciate her good looks and charm. But women feel the same way about their husbands. They want them to take care of themselves and to stay fit, clean, and groomed.

No woman wants to respond to a man who is sloppy, significantly overweight, and smells like he has been cleaning out the pig sties. Soap and water and a little aftershave go a long way toward making your body more attractive to your wife.

Jack wanted me to look nice. He was proud to have me with him when I was dressed up. He was disappointed when I didn't take the time to clean up for him.

One day after our fourth son was born, I had some rare extra time to work in the rose garden in the front yard of our little four-room house in Kingsburg, California. I spent about an hour pulling weeds and pruning back the bushes. I was dirty and sweaty, but when the boys woke up from their naps, I did not have time to take a shower. When Jack got home, he commented that he wished I was in a little better condition to greet him at the door.

The next day when he walked in the door after work, I was standing at the ironing board wearing a formal gown, high heels, and a tiara on my head. We both laughed as we realized how much we needed to understand each other's needs.

7. Give your wife time with other women.

As husbands, you are commanded to "live with your wives in an understanding way" (1 Peter 3:7). It is important for you to understand your wife—as best you can, and with God's help—both as a woman and as an individual with her own particular personality traits, strengths and weaknesses, talents, gifts, abilities, idiosyncrasies, and needs. However, there are some things about women that only other women can understand (the same can be said about men).

It's been said, "Men are from Mars and women are from Venus." We are different. We were made that way by God. Unisex was never God's intention. The Bible makes it very plain that "at the beginning of creation God made them 'male and female.'" (Mark 10:6).

Women's needs are different than men's. Their bodies have special cycles, they are more emotional, and often their thinking is poles apart from a man's.

A wise husband will give his wife time for herself and will create opportunities for her to get together with other women.

A few months after we were married, Jack noticed I had increasing resentment and anger toward our seminary situation—no money, no time, no family support, an unplanned pregnancy, a one-room apartment far away from campus, one car, and a stressful job. He would tell me, "You're out of fellowship! What you need is more time in the Word." (You can imagine my reaction to that advice.)

As Jack was praying for me (or "about" me), God spoke to him and made him aware of the needs I had that he could not meet. He heard of a get-together of first-year seminary wives that met twice a month for Bible study and fellowship. Knowing it would mean sacrificing a night at the library, he arranged for me to go. It was the beginning of a four-year relationship with three or four other wives, one of which has lasted even to this very day.

Getting together with these other women, all of us going through the same trials and struggles, helped me put my life in perspective and gave me the encouragement to continue. Hebrews 10:24 states, "And let us consider how we may spur one another on toward love and good deeds. Let us not give up meeting together, as some are in the habit of doing, but let us encourage one another."

When Mary discovered she was pregnant with baby Jesus, she was alarmed, anxious, and confused. She needed comfort and counseling, but instead of relying solely on Joseph to get her needs met, she went to Elizabeth, another woman, to reassure her and give her the faith to believe God and persevere.

Women need the encouragement and support of other women to "spur one another on toward love and good deeds." That is why older women are to teach and train the younger women to "love their husbands" (Titus 2:5).

Give your wife many opportunities to be with other women. Go to any expense to facilitate her time away from you and the children. It will pay off in the long run with a happier, more contented, and more submissive wife.

CHAPTER 17

Helpful Verses

❧

Commitment to the Word of God

Psalm 119:160—"*All your words are true.*" **Hebrews 6:18**—"*It is impossible for God to lie.*" We must be totally committed to God's Word as the only rule of faith and practice in our life.

John 8:32—"*You will know the truth, and the truth will make you free.*" No matter what the world says, God knows what is best for us. When we obey the truth of the Bible, it will set us free, not make us slaves.

1 Corinthians 2:5-7—"*That your faith might not rest on men's wisdom, but on God's power. We . . . speak a message of wisdom* *among the mature, but not the wisdom of this age."* The world, the flesh, and the devil will give us wrong views, philosophies, ideas, theories, and lies. God's Word is true wisdom and truth.

Psalm 119:105—*"Your word is a lamp to my feet and a light for my path."* We need light for each step we take as well as illumination as to where we should be going in the future. The Bible gives both.

Proverbs 13:13—*"He who scorns instruction will pay for it, but he who respects a command is rewarded."* We must respect God's Word and all He has to say to us. We never have to fear God's laws—He always blesses and rewards faithful obedience.

Hebrews 4:12—*"For the word of God is living and active. Sharper than any double-edged sword, it penetrates even to dividing soul and spirit, joints and marrow; it judges the thoughts and attitudes of the heart."* God is alive, and thus His Word is also very much alive, supernaturally revealing to us our own hearts, giving us accurate thoughts and insights about our lives, and convicting and encouraging us.

Understanding Marriage

Genesis 2:18—*"The LORD God said, 'It is not good for the man to be alone. I will make a helper suitable for him.'"* Unfallen man, with a flawless body, a perfect job, an ideal environment, and an intimate relationship with God, needed a wife. How much more our husbands! Marriage is a *ministry,* created by God for wives.

Proverbs 14:1—*"The wise woman builds her house, but with her own hands the foolish one tears hers down."* This is speaking of a wise wife—not necessarily a "happy" wife. A wise wife will build her husband's ego and self-esteem. She will build her relationship with her husband—a fool will destroy it. This implies that the wife has the ability to do either. A wise woman looks to the future and is willing to sacrifice to achieve a goal. A fool wants pleasure and happiness at the present time, without thought to the dire consequences of bad choices.

Ecclesiastes 5:4-5—*"When you make a vow to God, do not delay in fulfilling it. He has no pleasure in fools; fulfill your vow. It is better not to vow than to make a vow and not fulfill it."* We vowed to be faithful, "for better or worse," etc. Many of us make this vow, but we are really thinking, "for better or even better." Reread your marriage vows and take them seriously—God does.

Matthew 10:36—*"A man's enemies will be the members of his own household."* Often we have more difficulty with those we are closest to. We struggle most with those we love the most. Husbands, wives, family members, and in-laws can all work against the unity of a marriage.

1 Corinthians 7:3-4—*"The husband should fulfill his marital duty to his wife, and likewise the wife to her husband. The wife's body does not belong to her alone but also to her husband. In the same way, the husband's body does not belong to him alone but also to his wife."* We gave up our "rights" when we married our spouses. This isn't just talking about sexual fulfillment; it includes the physical presence in the home and "helping hand" that we need from each other.

Isaiah 9:6—*"For to us a child is born, to us a son is given, and the government will be on his shoulders. And he will be called Wonderful Counselor, Mighty God, Everlasting Father, Prince of Peace."* God's Son, Jesus, has been given to us to be the one who meets all our needs, needs that our husbands cannot meet. God never intended for our husbands to be the one to meet those needs for which He gave His Son. It is God who meets our needs. **Philippians 4:19**—*"My God will meet all your needs according to his glorious riches in Christ Jesus."* For our greatest need, salvation, Jesus paid it all. Through that one gift, our relationship with God has been restored, and we now have access to His throne of grace. What else do we really need? Isn't that enough?

Philippians 2:3-4—*"Do nothing out of selfish ambition or vain conceit, but in humility consider others better than yourselves. Each of you should look not only to your own interests, but also to the interests of others."* We are to take care of our husband's needs and look out for his interests before ourselves and over our needs or wants.

Romans 15:7—*"Accept one another, then, just as Christ accepted you, in order to bring praise to God."* We are not to have unrealistic expectations of our husband, or try to change him. We are to accept him as he is—weak, needy, and often hurting. That's how God accepts us.

Jeremiah 32:39—*"I will give them singleness of heart and action, so that they will always fear Me for their own good and the good of their children after them."* Unity and harmony in the home will not only be good for us, but for our children. God doesn't just think about what is best for us, but what is best for our children as well, and even for our children's children. **Psalm 103:17-18**—*"But from everlasting to everlasting the LORD's love is with those who fear Him, and His righteousness with their children's children—with those who keep His covenant and remember to obey His precepts."* God deals with us with future generations in mind. **Exodus 34:7**—*"The Lord, the compassionate and gracious God, slow to anger, abounding in love and faithfulness, maintaining love to thousands, and forgiving wickedness, rebellion and sin. Yet He does* not leave the guilty unpunished; He punishes the children and their children for the sin of the fathers to the third and fourth generation"

Proverbs 10:19—*"When words are many, sin is not absent, but he who holds his tongue is wise."* **Proverbs 21:23**—*"He who guards his mouth and his tongue keeps himself from calamity."* There is a reason we have the sayings, "Count to ten," or "Hold your tongue" when we're angry. Once words are spoken, they cannot be taken back.

Proverbs 20:3—*"It is to a man's honor to avoid strife, but every fool is quick to quarrel."* Quarreling dishonors us, and is for fools. **Proverbs 12:18**—*"Reckless words pierce like a sword, but the tongue of the wise brings healing."* Our words can hurt or heal.

Proverbs 20:22—*"Do not say, 'I'll pay you back for this wrong!' Wait for the* LORD, *and he will deliver you."* God will fight our battles for us in His own way and in His own time. We don't have to repay evil with evil when we are wronged in our marriage.

Proverbs 12:4—*"A wife of noble character is her husband's crown, but a disgraceful wife is like decay in his bones."* (NASB: *"She who shames him is like rottenness in his bones."*) A wife can either "make or break" her husband. To shame him, either publicly or privately, eats away his self-esteem and is like a cancer in his life. It will destroy him and his ministry. To criticize, ridicule, belittle, make fun of, etc., all destroys. A man who has "decay" in his bones cannot be the healthy, strong, whole, loving leader we want. **Proverbs 21:19**—*"Better to live in a desert than with a quarrelsome and ill-tempered wife."* Nagging destroys. **Proverbs 31:11-12**—*"The heart of her husband trusts in her . . . she does him good and not evil all the days of her life."* The Proverbs 31 woman was a businesswoman, powerful, independent, and free—but her first priority was her husband's welfare. God blessed her with a very fulfilling and successful life.

Colossians 3:13—"*Bear with each other and forgive whatever griev-ances you may have against one another. Forgive as the Lord forgave you.*" We are to bear with, endure, and tolerate our husband's faults as we desire for him to bear with our faults. Nobody is perfect, and every marriage is hard. Whatever he does that gives you grief, you are to forgive, just as the Lord forgives you. God has forgiven you much, you can forgive also. **Ephesians 4:32** (NASB)—"*Be kind to one another, tender-hearted, forgiving each other, just as God in Christ has forgiven you.*"

Proverbs 12:25—"*An anxious heart weighs a man down, but a kind word cheers him up.*" Our husband has the responsibility of providing for the family. This can be a great burden on him, and may give him many anxious moments. Our kindness, even if it's just a word, can cheer him up. **Job 6:14** (NASB)—"*For the despairing man there should be kindness from his friend; so that he does not forsake the fear of the Almighty.*" Both the husband and wife needs kindness to keep a close walk with the Lord. **Galatians 5:22-23**—"*But the fruit of the Spirit is love, joy, peace, patience, kindness, goodness, faithfulness, gentleness, and self-control.*" If you are filled with the Holy Spirit, you will show kindness to one another.

Proverbs 16:21 (NASB)—"*Sweetness of speech increases persua-siveness.*" A woman responds to kindness and can be persuaded to meet her husband's needs when he speaks to her sweetly. A wise wife will know when and how to speak to her husband. Nagging will never persuade.

Philippians 4:11—"*I have learned to be content whatever the circumstances.*" **1 Timothy 6:6**—"*But godliness with contentment is great gain.*" **Hebrews 13:5**—"*Keep your lives free from the love of money and be content with what you have, because God has said, 'Never will I leave you; never will I forsake you.'*" Cultivate contentment, realizing it is an attitude you have control over. Learn to be content with your circumstances, your situation, your husband, your house, your church. Realize that there are women around the world who have it much worse. Your husband loves a satisfied wife. Your children will be happier too, and they will follow your example to be content. The world is attracted to contented people. It is a powerful testimony.

Proverbs 21:9—*"It is better to live in a corner of a roof than in a house shared with a contentious woman."* The point is that discontent—which causes nagging because of the lack of things, beautiful houses, or money—is not worth it. Better to live with little in peace than with abundance but in debt.

Philippians 4:8—*"Whatever is true, whatever is noble, whatever is right, whatever is pure, whatever is lovely, whatever is admirable—if anything is excellent or praiseworthy—think about such things."* Think of your husband's good qualities and dwell on them; they are the reasons you married him in the first place. Praise him for them. Be thankful. Develop a positive attitude, rather than a negative one. Recognize that a critical and complaining spirit is evil and destructive. **"Praise the good—pray the bad."**

Ephesians 5:33 (NASB)—*"The wife must see to it that she respects her husband."* The husband was created with the need for authority and the respect that the position of leader in the home requires. Admiration and esteem, building up a man's ego, makes him a better husband, father, and leader. It doesn't have anything to do with his worthiness—none of us are worthy of the blessings God gives us. It has to do with our role as helper to meet a husband's needs. Most affairs start because a woman admires a man, shows him respect, and makes him feel good around her—like the way we treated our husbands before we married them. But a wife often stops this behavior after marriage and makes the husband feel awful around her. God says, *"You fool!"* (Proverbs 14:1).

Psalm 142:2—*"I pour out my complaint before him; before him I tell my trouble."* It is good to complain to God if it prevents us from complaining to others. God knows our heart, and he wants us to "pour out your hearts to Him, for God is our refuge" (Psalm 62:8). David poured out his heart to God, telling him all that he was thinking and feeling, and said some pretty bad things about his enemies. But God never rebuked his honesty in prayer. In fact, He called David "a man after my own heart." God is the only one who can change our heart and the heart of our husband. Talk to God a lot about your marriage, your ministry, your problems. Complain to God, not to your husband or others. Pray it—don't say it!

Psalm 1:3—*"[S]he is like a tree planted by streams of water, which yields its fruit in season."* We must recognize that we all have seasons of life, as well as times of the month. We shouldn't expect to be able to do what others do who may be in a different season of life. **Romans 12:6**—*"We have different gifts, according to the grace given us."* We are also all given different gifts, and therefore will respond differently to any situation or problem. Many husbands and wives have been given different gifts, strengths, and talents, which are good and planned by God. We should celebrate these differences rather than make them a source of friction.

John 14:2 (NASB)—*"In My Father's house are many dwelling places; if it were not so, I would have told you; for I go to prepare a place for you."* This world is not our home. It is a fallen world. It will never be perfect. God never intended for us to stay here. We can be patient for "a little while" (compared to eternity) until we get the ideal home that Jesus Himself is preparing for us. So when you desire things you can't afford, say to yourself, "Someday I'll have that, and that, and that, and one of those..."

In Summary

1 Peter 3:8-11 (NLT)—*"Finally, all of you should be of one mind, full of sympathy toward each other, loving one another with tender hearts and humble minds. Don't repay evil for evil. Don't retaliate when people say unkind things about you. Instead, pay them back with a blessing. That is what God wants you to do, and he will bless you for it. For the Scriptures say,*
'If you want a happy life and good days,
keep your tongue from speaking evil,
and keep your lips from telling lies.
Turn away from evil and do good;
work hard at living in peace with others.'"

These verses are all in the context of marriage. If we could follow just these four verses, our marriages would be a blessing for us and others. We all "want a happy life and good days." We want strong marriages and families. These verses say that we need to do two things:

1. Watch what we say.
2. Do the right thing.

Simple to say—extremely hard to do. But most people know when they are saying things that are not loving or are unkind. And most of us know right from wrong. Jesus did the right thing when He died on the cross even when He didn't want to. We are to follow His example (see 1 Peter 2:21-24). *"That is what God wants you to do, and he will bless you for it."*

Acknowledgments

MY MOTIVATION for this book is to help other wives who are struggling in their marriages, who may have given up hope, or who may need to encourage their family and friends who need to hear these truths that God has taught me. Better yet, I hope to help countless of young woman who have not yet chosen their mates, to help them know what husbands need before they become wives, and to give them a biblical foundation for their ministry of marriage.

As I noted at the beginning, I did not want to write this book. However, I have been asked by women across the country and literally around the world to put my talks into writing. I can connect with my audience when I see their faces, hear their laughter, even see the tears welling up in the eyes of those who have "been there, done that." Putting it in writing is much more of a challenge. It was only the constant urging from women across the world to whom I have spoken that gave me the motivation to sit at my laptop hours on end, typing out words.

I would not have even attempted this project, much less sit at my laptop, hours on end, typing out words, without the expertise of my son, Dean, who is a writer and successful author and the editor and publisher for this work. (Check out his latest book at www.oldmoneynewsouth.com—a shameless plug from Mom.)

My deepest love and gratitude goes to my family. Mark, Brian, Arny, and Dean, you have become amazing and remarkable men, in spite of the failures of a mother who didn't love your father the way he needed me to. Your care and devotion in this new chapter of life has kept me from loneliness and fear.

Tricia, Lori, and Jan, I love you for loving me and my sons—and for being wonderful mothers to my grandchildren.

Hunter, Kasey, Morgan, Duncan, Corey, Devon, Jacki, Jordan, David, Given, Tabitha, and Jaime—you have brought me more joy than you can imagine. To watch you all grow in your love for me, your family, your cousins, and your God overwhelms my heart.

Gary, you are the patriarch of the Arnold family now. You and Kay have loved me as a true sister, not as a sister-in-law. Polly, you amaze me with your spunk and spirit, and inspire me to also live to be an active 90-year-old.

Nancy and Jony, we have always been different, but I love and admire you both.

All the family at Equipping Pastors International has given Jack, and now me, tremendous support and confidence to continue the privilege of training pastors and wives around the world. Thank you, Don and Merril, Bob, Chuck, Diana, Dale, Dan, Ron, Doug, Mary Ann, and Bob.

This book would be 500 pages if I thanked all those who have encouraged me over the years. But I do want to thank Larry and Carole, Tom and Becky, Bob and Barb, Don and Ida, Johnny and Dawn, Jim and Ginny, and Dennis and Cindy. You have opened your hearts and homes to me.

Arch and Joyce, Robert and Kim, Ruth and Becky, your friendship, encouragement, and concern is a gift from God.

Susan, Barbara, Carolyn, Pam, and Jane, your example of servant leadership and godly wisdom has been a model of true womanhood and has given me confidence to follow in your footsteps.

Jim Fitzgerald and Mike Beates, you are not only my pastors but great pals, comrades, and fellow travelers with hearts for Africa.

Bob and Sunny, this book would have a different ending were it not for your continued love, exhortation, friendship, and fun over the many years we have known each other. You told me what I needed to hear, as "the pleasantness of one's friend springs from his earnest counsel" (Proverbs 27:9). And when I wanted to throw in the towel, you kept me going. "If one falls down, his friend can help him up. But pity the man who falls and has no one to help him up!" (Ecclesiastes 4:10).

‡

My heart is filled with love and appreciation for Jack, who hung in there with me for over forty-seven years when he didn't always receive the care, concern, and admiration he needed from me. He is now basking in true love and enjoying his rewards after hearing, "Well done, my good and faithful servant."

My greatest thanks go to God, who graciously showed mercy upon me, drawing me to Himself, enabling me to see the truth not just with my eyes but with my heart, and allowing me to experience the true joy and fulfillment that being a helpful wife brings. My love for Jack abounded when I gained biblical knowledge of the ministry of marriage, when God gave me insight into my role as a helper, and when I learned that God knows best.

"And this is my prayer [for you, dear reader], that your love may abound more and more in knowledge and depth of insight so that you may be able to discern what is best" (Philippians 1:8-9).

About the Author

CAROL ARNOLD was born in Hollywood and sailed across the Pacific at age ten to the tropical island of Guam. She had nine different animals for pets, including a goat, a pig, and a fuzzy fruit bat known as a "flying fox" that Carol called Charlie.

As a teenager, she took a two-week trip alone, leaving Guam to attend the University of California at Los Angeles (UCLA), in the city where her grandparents helped found the Hollywood Bowl and promoted socialism and the sexual revolution before it was cool.

Carol speaks to women, church leaders, and pastors and their wives as cofounder of Equipping Pastors International. She has traveled to every continent, but Africa is now her main focus of ministry.

When she is not visiting others, they are visiting her from across America and from all over the world at her home near Orlando, Florida, where she loves to entertain friends and family. She keeps a fresh batch of her famous homemade cookies in the kitchen. The key is under the wreath.

You can e-mail Carol at DoctorJLA@hotmail.com